Trail of the Coeur d'Alenes Unofficial Guidebook

And the 300k Bitterroot Loop

2015

by
Estar Holmes

Acknowledgement

This is the eighth edition of the *Trail of the Coeur d'Alenes Unofficial Guidebook*. The guide includes tips on riding the entire 300k Bitterroot Loop, as signed and mapped by the Friends of the Coeur d'Alene Trails. The loop comprises the Trail of the Coeur d'Alenes and the Route of the Hiawatha non-motorized trails, Northern Pacific and Milwaukee multi-use rail beds, and a 13-mile stretch of state highway.

This guide is a cooperative venture supported by more than seventy advertisers, book vendors, and information providers. My heartfelt thanks to all who participate in making the guide and related Web sites possible. Special thanks to Russ Davis of Gray Dog Press in Spokane, Washington, for his dedication in getting the book printed and distributed.

Cover Photograph: Overview of Wallace, Idaho, by John Darrington. Inserts by Estar Holmes: Nancy and Mike Merickel riding their tandem cycle around the Center of the Universe in Wallace, Idaho; Mining Family Statue at Mining Heritage Exhibit, Wallace, Idaho; Spaceship sighted at The Red Light Garage.

Other Photo & Model Credits: Photos on pgs. 3, 4, and 5 courtesy Margie Cantlon. Photo of Springston Trailhead, pg. 38, by Isaac Holmes. Photos of Silver Mountain Bike Park, pgs. 52 and 61, by Matt Vielle Photography ©2014 by permission of Silver Mountain; Photo of Silver Rapids Water Park, pg. 52, courtesy of Silver Mountain; Photo of 1313 Club of Wallace, ID, pg. 79, provided by Dean Cooper; Paul and Pat Aniotzbehere at Pulaski Trail, pg. 76. Photo of G.F. Smith cabin on pg. 43, courtesy of Historic Wallace Preservation Society, Inc.

Photography, graphic design, and book layout by Estar Holmes.

Enjoy many more pictures of the area traversed by the Bitterroot Loop at pinterest.com/bitterrootloop. You are encouraged to post pictures and comments about your rail-trail experiences on the *Trail of Coeur d'Alenes Riders* Facebook page. See what's happening on the Bitterroot Loop at facebook.com/Historic.Bitterroot.Loop. For updates on live music and lodgings in the greater south Lake CdA reagion, go to southlakecda.com.

Trail of he Coeur d'Alenes Unofficial Guidebook 2015
© 2015, South Lake Promotions, Inc., PO Box 185, Harrison, ID 83833

Published by
Gray Dog Press
Spokane, Washington
www.graydogpress.com
ISBN: 978-1-936178-94-0

Contents

Welcome
to North Idaho's
Trail of the Coeur d'Alenes
and the 300k Bitterroot Loop

THIS TRAIL HAS BEEN INDUCTED INTO

The Rail-Trail Hall of Fame

rails-to-trails
conservancy

www.railstotrails.org

Congratulations on your decision to check out the world-class Trail of the Coeur d'Alenes and connecting trails of North Idaho's 300k Bitterroot Loop. This guide is designed to help you plan your trip and enrich appreciation of the areas traversed by the trails. Annual publication of the guide began in 2008 as a resource for visitors along the 72-mile Trail of the Coeur d'Alenes. The rest of the Bitterroot Loop was added after Friends of the Coeur d'Alene Trails linked and mapped four rail bed trails under the name of Bitterroot Loop, which was featured by the Rails to Trails Conservancy magazine in 2010. When hundreds of cyclists started showing up on remote mountain roads, the Bitterroot Loop trails were added to the guide to inform visitors what to expect along the way.

Most of the 300k loop is in the northern Idaho panhandle, with a short section in western Montana. The loop links the Trail of the Coeur d'Alenes, the Northern Pacific Route (Nor-Pac), Route of the Hiawatha (RoH), Milwaukee Scenic and Alternate Routes, and a 13-mile segment of rural highway along Idaho State Route-5 (SR-5).

Information for the guide is gathered by riding the trails, visiting communities, touring amenities, experiencing services, and otherwise keeping up on what's new. Visitors who want to stay beyond two or three days of rail-trail riding are offered Connecting Trips selected for convenience of access and unique offerings.

Driving directions to trailheads and trailside communities are provided from I-90 because most people come with cycles strapped to their vehicles. This guide, however, aims to serve visitors traveling by cycle, so the primary focus is on amenities that are conveniently located within one mile of the trails. Also included are services that are an easy ride from the main trails, or where courtesy shuttles are offered. Suggestions are included on ways to reach trailside destinations from as far away as the Spokane International Airport by using a combination of dedicated cycling trails and public or private transport. Alternatives to riding in traffic are offered wherever possible.

What's in this book?

After this introduction, see answers to **Frequently Asked Questions** and a **map** that shows where the Bitterroot Loop trails and **Connecting Trips** are situated. That's followed by descriptions of **trailheads, wayside stops,** and trailside **community tours,** interspersed with historical **points of interest.** Trailheads are listed in a clockwise direction starting at Plummer. Find quick references to resource suppliers starting at pg. 110, including **lodging and camping, rental shops,** and **transportation** services. This is also where to find phone numbers of trail managers and other official contacts. For Web page links to lodgings and restaurants go to **southlakecda.com/trail.htm.**

People may wonder why certain business services are included, or embellished upon, while others receive scant mention or none at all. Attractions, activities, and amenities that appear on the writer's radar, and seem interesting or useful to visitors, are included. Most years, new businesses open after the book goes to print. Each year, businesses support research, printing, and distribution of this guide through modest advertising investments. Their contributions are necessary to provide detailed information cycle visitors need about features and services along the Bitterroot Loop trails. Think of them as squeaky wheels that generally receive more attention than those who don't return phone calls, pay bills, or otherwise have no interest in supporting the project. When making travel plans, please consider doing business with those who reach out to you by supporting this book and related Web sites. One goal of the publisher (a local rural microenterprise) is to meet production and distribution costs while keeping the retail price at $9.95 for as long as possible, so number of pages is a consideration as well. Comments from the cycling community largely influence what goes in or comes out. Visitors are encouraged to share their observations and insights on the Trail of the Coeur d'Alenes Riders Facebook page, or they can contact me privately via the information on the back of the title page.

Trail Conditions

The Trail of the Coeur d'Alenes is a well-maintained 72-mile ribbon of asphalt that spans the Idaho Panhandle from Plummer to Mullan. The rest of the Bitterroot Loop trails are packed dirt and gravel, with the exception of the 13-mile stretch on State Route 5 from St. Maries to Heyburn Park.

The Trail of the Coeur d'Alenes is mostly flat except for 7-mile spans on either end. The approximate 5% grade between Plummer and Heyburn Park, and on Chatcolet Bridge, are the steepest parts. The overall gain from Lake Coeur d'Alene's shore to Mullan, Idaho, is about 1,100 feet over a span of 60 miles. The most dramatic elevation changes occur on the NorPac section of the Bitterroot Loop between Mullan and Lookout Pass, where the trail climbs 1,461 feet in a little under 11 miles. Then the 37 miles between Lookout Pass and Avery descends 2,300 feet. On the RoH, a shuttle bus is available for the 1.7% incline back up the 15 mile-stretch between Pearson and Roland Trailheads.

If riding the entire loop, bring a hybrid or mountain bike, or plan to rent one. Pack a repair kit and spare tubes. Helmets and lights are mandatory on the Hiawatha. The lights will be useful in other tunnels along the way as well. Be prepared for overnight wilderness survival in case of a mishap. Cell phone service is spotty along many areas. Some lodgings include free land line calls and there are a few pay phones along the way, so put a prepaid phone card in the survival kit.

Connecting Trips

The guide focuses on the needs of visitors touring by cycle, so emphasis is on facilities within one mile of the trails. However, *Connecting Trips* with fun amenities and interesting lodgings are featured if they are within an easy ride from the Bitterroot Loop or accessible by courtesy shuttle or gondola.

Historic

Trails that comprise the Bitterroot Loop all lie within a portion of the aboriginal homeland of the Coeur d'Alene Tribe of Indians, originally called *Schitsu'umsh*, loosely translated as The People Found Here. The Trail of the Coeur d'Alenes follows the former Union Pacific rail line that crosses ancient paths where the First People walked, and cuts through spectacular scenery traversed by mountain men, fur traders, Jesuit missionaries, soldiers, homesteaders, and fortune hunters who began arriving in the mid 1800s. Bitterroot Loop trails connect rural communities that boomed when gold and silver were discovered, where miners, loggers, and entrepreneurs—many of them first generation immigrants—flocked with hopes of better lives.

The Trail of the Coeur d'Alenes is paved, well-maintained, and mostly flat for 72 miles

Visitors who enjoy history will find many stories along the trails in the form of guided tours, museums, interpretive signs, and books by local authors, many of which contrast the optimism of hopeful settlers with the harshness of daily life during North Idaho's gold rush and early 20th Century homesteading. Murals, old photographs, and artifacts are displayed on the walls of businesses and public buildings all along the Loop, and visitors are invited to drop in to have a look.

Point of Interest: The first known encounter of *Schitsu'umsh* and white men occurred when a few of the tribe's members were visiting Nez Perce country during the Lewis & Clark expedition to the Pacific Ocean. They told some of the explorers about their land and the great lake that is its center piece. Over the next decades scattered hunters and trappers filtered into the tribe's territory, but nobody can say exactly when they arrived. In 1842, the Catholic missionary, Father Pierre DeSmet, S.J., built a log chapel near a tribal camp on the northern shore of Lake Coeur d'Alene at *Nchim Kinkw*, which means, Head of the Water.

The *Schitsu'umsh* had long expected the arrival of the priests since Chief Circling Raven had prophesied a century earlier that men with black robes and crossed sticks would come in peace with strong medicine. The need for strong medicine was critical since waves of smallpox were ravaging the people and traditional healers were powerless against the deadly plagues. Smallpox was introduced to the tribe in the 1700s, it is believed, by contact with hunters from the Great Plains after horses were introduced here, and the Black Robes were expected to bring a cure.

Protocol

The people of rural north Idaho are generally friendly, hospitable, hard working, and conservative. (The colloquialism "north Idaho" is preferred over "northern" Idaho). They consider resource extraction a necessity for a quality life, and they may remind you they cut the trees and mine the metals that everyone uses. They carry guns, hunt, fish, and are extremely proud and protective of their heritage. Do not be alarmed if you see somebody with a rifle strapped to their back, cruising down main street on an ATV with a dead animal draped across the hood. Chances are good they are not a terrorist, but a normal north Idaho resident doing what is perfectly respectable around here.

The locals remember the familiar sound of trains rumbling through and the plaintive sound of their whistles blowing. Trains meant goods were moving, money was being made, and people were working and able to provide for their families. The trains represent a nostalgic time when life was good.

These days the Inland Northwest is a die hard motor culture. People love their quads, snowmobiles, SUVs, and pickup trucks — the bigger the better. The motorized locals are not accustomed to sharing "their" roads with cycles so don't be surprised if they are not thrilled about having to slow down for you. It's not your fault that the roads have no shoulders, but most motorists will figure there is something wrong with *you* if they have to swerve to get past you. That's why this book is written to help cyclists travel on trails as much as possible. If you opt for a highway route, consider using a rear view mirror and hugging the edge of the road.

Also, while on the topic of protocol, word on the street is some business owners are saying too many cyclists expect to use their restrooms or ask to have their water bottles refilled without offering anything in return. So, unless otherwise noted, to keep from giving all cyclists a bad name, those who want free services should stick to using public facilities, many of which are mentioned in this guide.

A Constant State of Change

Businesses in rural north Idaho tend to be like wild mushrooms in that they come and go rather quickly. (The dainty fungus specimen at right was found along the north bank of the St. Joe River). This guide attempts to keep up with the changing business landscape, but they close, move, start up, or change hands after publication. So, to stay safe and happy, it's best not to assume anything. Call ahead and remain flexible. Also, weather events may very occasionally require sections of trail to close temporarily. To check conditions call headquarters at 208.682.3814 during business hours.

✴ The Trail of the Coeur d'Alenes and Connecting Trips ✪ on the 300k Bitterroot Loop

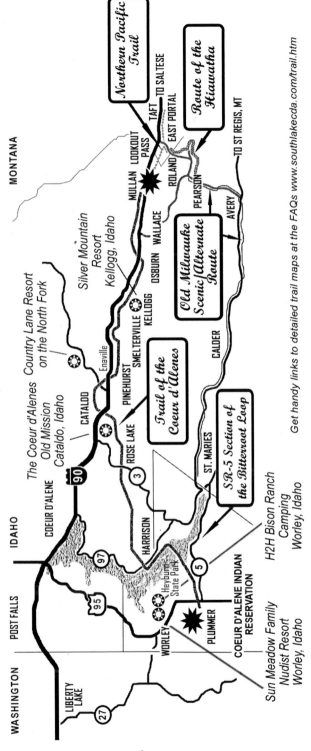

Northern Pacific Trail

Route of the Hiawatha

Old Milwaukee Scenic/Alternate Route

Trail of the Coeur d'Alenes

SR-5 Section of the Bitterroot Loop

MONTANA

WASHINGTON

IDAHO

COEUR D'ALENE INDIAN RESERVATION

LIBERTY LAKE

POST FALLS

COEUR D'ALENE

WORLEY

PLUMMER

HARRISON

ST. MARIES

ROSE LAKE

CATALDO

PINEHURST

SMELTERVILLE

KELLOGG

OSBURN

WALLACE

MULLAN

LOOKOUT PASS

TAFT

TO SALTESE

EAST PORTAL

ROLAND

PEARSON

AVERY

CALDER

TO ST REGIS, MT

Silver Mountain Resort Kellogg, Idaho

Country Lane Resort on the North Fork

The Coeur d'Alenes Old Mission Cataldo, Idaho

Enaville

Heyburn State Park

H2H Bison Ranch Camping Worley, Idaho

Sun Meadow Family Nudist Resort Worley, Idaho

Get handy links to detailed trail maps at the FAQs www.southlakecda.com/trail.htm

- 6 -

WHERE DOES THE TRAIL START?

Some say the trail starts in Mullan, Idaho, near the Montana border. Others consider Plummer, near the Washington state line, the beginning. This guide starts in Plummer for several reasons: The trail mile markers go from west to east; *Hn'ya(pqi'nn*, the Plummer trailhead, is closest to Spokane (the largest city between Seattle and Chicago); The Coeur d'Alene Tribe's headquarters are in Plummer, and both local history and the trail's establishment start with them. But with 19 trailheads, you can decide where your adventure begins.

HOW DO I GET TO THE TRAILHEADS?

Driving directions are provided from I-90 to each trailhead. Are you traveling without a vehicle? The FAQ: *How Do I Get to the Trail Without Driving?* explins how to reach the trail without a car, while avoiding riding in traffic as much as possible. *Get to the Trails Without Driving* in the *Bitterroot Loop Service Providers* section has ideas for private transportation options that will get you and your gear to a trailhead. Guests at the **Wallace Inn** may arrange for pick up by a paid shuttle from Spokane International Airport. Guests at the **Pines Motel** and **Fort Hemenway Manor** in St. Maries may request a courtesy shuttle between their lodgings and Heyburn State Park. Other possibilities include engaging a local tour company or shuttle service.

HOW MUCH DOES IT COST TO RIDE THE TRAIL?

Riding the Trail of the Coeur d'Alenes is free. There are donation tubes at Medimont, Bull Run, Cataldo, Enaville, and Mullan for those who would like to show their appreciation. There is no charge for parking at trailheads, except at Heyburn State Park, where it costs $5 per day, per vehicle. Idaho residents can get an annual pass for $10 when registering their vehicles, good at any state park for one year. Those who already registered vehicles but did not buy a park sticker can do so at any Idaho DMV. Nonresidents can buy an annual pass for $40.

Idaho resident veterans with a 100% service-related disability can apply for a lifetime Veteran's Pass that waives parking and basic camping fees. Get an application at any state park, park regional service center, or go online to parksandrecreation.idaho.gov/activities/camping click on *Discounts and Fees* in the left column. Then see *Idaho*

Disabled Veterans and click *Apply Today*. This takes you to a brochure with the application. Print, fill out, and fax or send it to the address provided, along with a letter from the Idaho Department of Veteran's Affairs, affirming your disability. Call Heyburn State Park during business hours if you have questions about park fees: 208.686.1308.

ARE GROUP PERMITS REQUIRED?

Yes. Groups of 25 or more are required to contact a trail manager to request a permit. Additionally, any group wishing to host a special event or commercial activity on the trail must have authorization from trail managers. Find their phone numbers under: *Information About Area Cycle Trails* in the *Bitterroot Loop Service Providers* section.

HOW LONG DOES IT TAKE TO RIDE THIS TRAIL?

If you are in a big hurry, you can race across the Idaho Panhandle and back in a day. If you relish back country discoveries and moving in rural time, you can find enough to do and see to spend a relaxing and memorable week vacationing along the trail.

ARE TOURS AVAILABLE?

ROW Adventures offers a selection of trail tours by knowledgeable, certified guides, daily from June 1 through August 31. Options include one day tours; 5-day package deals with a cycling, rafting, and kayaking mix; and full logistical support for self-guided trail vacations. See *Local Trail Touring Service* on page 110.

WHAT ELSE IS THERE TO DO?

Hike, boat, float, kayak, stand up paddle, geocache, fish, mountain bike, swim, zipline, sight-see, taste wine, sip microbrews, dance, sing, golf, and more. Find things to do under each trailhead description, and check out the Connecting Trips for more ideas. Bike rides from the rail-trails into the surrounding back country are documented by volunteers at: friendsofcdatrails.org/other_trails.html.

WHERE CAN I GET TRAIL MAPS?

Friends of the Coeur d'Alene Trails distributes maps to area businesses and visitor centers. You may also download a PDF online or contact the Friends to request a map by mail. Find them at friendsofcdatrails.org or snail mail them at Box 804, Wallace, ID, 83873. The Friends map shows the entire 300k Bitterroot Loop. The State of

Idaho provides an online map of the Trail of the Coeur d'Alenes only. It's also there in three segments that are printable on standard-sized paper. Easily find links to downloadable maps provided by both the Friends group and Idaho State Parks at southlakecda.com/trail. Look for the FAQ: *Where Can I Get a Map?* and click "maps."

WHERE CAN I RENT BICYCLES?

Quality bicycle rentals are available along the Trail of the Coeur d'Alenes in **Harrison** and **Kellogg**, and on the Bitterroot Loop at **The Bike Shop at Hughes Ace** in St. Maries. You can find details about these shops and the cycles they specialize in under trailhead community descriptions, and quickly access their phone numbers in the *Service Providers* section.

If Coeur d'Alene is your base for exploring north Idaho's trails, head for **Terra Sports** downtown on Sherman Ave. The staff are fellow cycle enthusiasts who will fit your bike to you and share insider tips on the area's routes and rides. Choose from hybrid or road bikes, tandems, child trailers, or trail-a-bike. Bike rentals come with helmets, maps, locks, bottle cages, a copy of Idaho bike laws, and seat bags. User-friendly bike racks that fit most cars and trucks are available. If you buy a bike at Terra Sports they will package it and ship it home for you.

CAN I PITCH A TENT ALONG THE TRAIL?

Tents are only allowed along the trail at designated campgrounds. Several full service campgrounds are located on, or within a few blocks of the trail at: Heyburn State Park, Harrison, Cataldo, Kingston, Pinehurst, Osburn, and Wallace. See details about these and RV-only

parking under trailhead listings. See back of book for phone numbers and southlakecda.com/trail.htm for links to campground Web sites.

ARE BONFIRES ALLOWED ALONG THE TRAIL?

Bonfires are only allowed at designated camping areas.

WHAT ABOUT LODGING?

There is a wide selection of lodgings and price ranges along the Trail of the Coeur d'Alenes, from rustic budget cabins to high end condos. You can find some really good deals on lodgings. Plan carefully along the rest of the Bitterroot Loop because it's rural and remote with overnight accommodations about 25 miles or more apart.

WHAT KIND OF FOOD CAN I EXPECT ON THE TRAIL?

Trailside restaurants offer American, Mexican, Chinese, and Italian food. You will also encounter rural expanses without any services at all. There are no vegetarian restaurants on the trail, but most provide a few meatless choices. The few selections of wild, organic, vegetarian, vegan, gluten-free, or locally grown options are noted under each trailhead listing. Quite a few restaurants make food from scratch with fresh ingredients and bake fresh daily. Wild huckleberries are prolific in the Northwest, and you will find a wide variety of treats made from berries picked in the surrounding mountains. H2H Bison Ranch provides locally raised bison to a few restaurants. But fresh, locally grown menu items are an exception, not the rule on the loop. See southlakecda.com/trail.htm for a list of restaurants with menus online.

DO TRAILHEADS HAVE DRINKING WATER?

Trailheads and wayside stops don't have drinking water, with the exception of the fountain at Hn'ya(pqi'nn (Plummer) Trailhead. The only other water source that can be considered as "belonging to the trail," is a spigot east of Smelterville at the state-owned shop next to the trail. Stretches between water sources vary from one to 25 miles, so plan ahead and stock up when you can. You will ride along creeks, rivers, and lakes most of the way, but heavy metals from years of mining activity still wash into the drainage. Boiling this water in an attempt to purify it will just further concentrate metals.

ARE RESTROOMS OPEN ALL YEAR?

Flush toilets at Hn'ya)pqi'nn Trailhead in Plummer shut down during cold weather to avoid damage from freezing. Vault toilets are open all year. Portable toilets at Cataldo and Mullan Trailheads are removed at the end of summer. There is no restroom at the trailhead in Wallace. Please use facilities at the Chamber of Commerce Visitor Center, the Northern Pacific Depot Museum, or Wallace District Mining Museum. Avoid using restrooms in businesses unless you intend to make a purchase.

ARE HELMETS REQUIRED?

Helmets are not legally required on the Trail of the Coeur d'Alenes. They are mandatory on the Hiawatha.

HOW LONG MAY I PARK AT TRAILHEADS?

You may park long enough to ride the trail, except at Smelterville Trailhead, where overnight parking is banned. Expect an extra fee at Chatcolet Trailhead.

IS THERE RV PARKING AT TRAILHEADS?

There are no designated RV parking spots at trailheads, but several have room to park and maneuver large rigs conveniently. These include: Plummer, Chatcolet, Silver Mountain, and Mullan. State and private RV parks close to the trails accommodate RVs at Heyburn, Harrison, Rose Lake, Cataldo, Enaville, Pinehurst, Kellogg, Osburn, Wallace, Lookout Pass, and along the St. Joe River. Find details under individual trailhead listings. See phone numbers under *Service Providers* and campground links at southlakecda.com/trail.htm.

WILL MY STUFF BE SAFE IN MY CAR AT TRAILHEADS?

There are no guarantees. This is a low-crime area, but lock valuables out of sight, just as you would anywhere. Police and sheriffs patrol trailheads in their jurisdictions. Contact officials in the jurisdictions listed in the back of the book if you want specific information.

IS THERE CELL PHONE COVERAGE?

Verizon and ATT cover the region with varying degrees of success. Service is spotty on the remote portions of the trail along the Coeur d'Alene River. Riders on the Bitterroot Loop should expect no service in the St. Joe River drainage to within about 10 miles of St. Maries.

IS THE TRAIL SAFE FOR WOMEN ALONE?

Women should take the same precautions as they do whenever traveling alone in a remote area.

CAN I BRING MY DOG?

Pets are welcome if they remain on a short leash and under your control at all times. Please clean up any "land mines" they deposit.

CAN I BRING MY HORSE?

Horses are not allowed on the trail.

WHAT IS THE BEST SEASON TO RIDE?

Some riders come as soon as the snow melts, but most visit during late spring, summer, and early autumn. If you crave solitude, ride in spring or fall. The scent of blooming wildflowers is a big treat in spring. However, some businesses may still be in winter hibernation or on seasonal hours then. To experience everything trailside communities have to offer, come between Memorial and Labor Days. Summertime temperatures are generally pleasant, but there can be scorchers reaching into the 100s. October offers a spectacular display of vibrant colors, and average Indian summer temperatures are in the high 50s to low 60s. Winter conditions vary wildly in north Idaho from year to year. But snow generally starts around Thanksgiving and stays until March. There may be brief snowstorms in April or even May.

IS THERE CROSS-COUNTRY SKIING?

You are welcome to ski on the trail. The amount of snow varies from year to year and location on the trail. The parks department sets track around Smelterville when conditions allow. It snows more between Wallace and Mullan, and this section is shared with snowmobiles. Call 208.682.3814 for updates.

CAN I GET HELP IF I CRASH MY BIKE?

If a mishap renders your bike inoperable, what should you do?

Jason Brown of the Coeur d'Alene Tribe's Recreation Department says, "I would view those types of issues similar to hiking in a remote area. You should always go with someone else in the event something happens, so that person can go for help." That's good advice, but if you decide to ride alone anyway, keep this guide with you. It lists telephone numbers of transportation companies and trail managers you can call if you happen to be at a spot with cell service. If someone is hurt, dial 9-1-1. Otherwise, you're on your own or at the mercy of a kind passerby. Or, you can ride with peace of mind by hiring **ROW Adventures**, which offers self-guided trail vacations with full, 24-hour logistical support.

Some people have crashed into the **bollards** that are placed at crossroads to warn of possible vehicle traffic. Note the squiggly white lines before them and the stop signs on them. To avoid slamming into a bollard or being hit by a car, it's best to slow down and stop.

IS THE TRAIL ADA ACCESSIBLE?

Trailheads have marked disabled parking spaces and most have accessible restrooms, except for the portable potties at three trailheads. Please refer to trailhead descriptions for details.

ARE MOTORIZED VEHICLES ALLOWED?

The CdA Trail is non-motorized with the exception of a multi-use section between Wallace and Mullan, open to snowmobiles during winter. You will occasionally encounter official trail vehicles along the way. Motorized wheelchairs are freely allowed on the trail. Anyone with a disability who wants to use another type of motorized device, such as an electric bike, needs a permit. Go in person to Heyburn Park, the Old Mission, or the Coeur d'Alene Tribe, and ask for the trail manager. There is no charge for the permit, but you will be required to indicate you are disabled. Call first to inquire what devices are allowed and to make sure someone is available to issue the permit.

WHAT WILDLIFE IS THERE?

Much of the trail is rural, and one of its charms is the presence of wild animals. Eagle, osprey, blue heron, deer, beaver, snake, turtle, turkey, moose, coyote, bear, elk, and cougar all live in the region. Do not attempt to feed or otherwise befriend any wild animals. If you see a cute little baby do not try to pet it. Assume a protective mother is nearby ready to attack you. Give all wild animals plenty of room to get away from you. Please report bear, cougar, or moose sightings within the Coeur d'Alene Indian Reservation to the tribal wildlife program by calling 208.686.6603. You may call trail managers on weekdays to get updates on animal sightings and any other trail information that involves your safety.

WHAT'S WITH THOSE WARNING SIGNS?

Heavy metals from more than a century of mining are still being isolated and cleaned up in the Coeur d'Alene River drainage. Several factors contribute to their presence: Mining companies did not historically isolate tailings from the environment, so they wash down through the Coeur d'Alene River drainage; portions of the rail bed were built with mine waste; and, ore sometimes spilled from passing trains. The asphalt strip, basalt armoring, gravel, and plants along the trail are there to cover metals remaining in the soil. The EPA has declared the trail safe for public use. Many locals are convinced there was never a danger in the first place, and that the federal government is blowing things out of proportion for its own sinister ends. The view on the Coeur d'Alene Reservation is different. The tribe insisted on removal of all contaminants feasible from along the railroad grade.

HOW DO I GET TO THE TRAIL WITHOUT DRIVING?

This FAQ is for cycle travelers coming from as far as Spokane International Airport, who want to get to the trail while avoiding riding in traffic as much as possible. The easiest way is to hire **ROW Adventures** to handle all the logistics for you. See *Getting to the Trails Without Driving* in the **Service Providers** section for more information.

Guests who lodge at the **Wallace Inn** also have an easy solution. They may request a paid shuttle, for themselves and their cycles, from Spokane International Airport to the motel. Shuttle arrangements must be made at least two weeks in advance of the needed date.

The Spokane and North Idaho Centennial Trails will get you between Spokane and Coeur d'Alene with minimal street riding. But no bike trails link the City of Coeur d'Alene with the Trail of the Coeur d'Alenes, about 30 miles away. To stay off the highways, you can take free CityLink buses or hire a land or boat shuttle.

Spokane Airport Express shuttles people and cycles to and from anywhere in the region, so don't let the "airport" part of their name stop you from calling. It is best to provide at least two days advance notice if possible, and more if you have a large group. However, they will try to accommodate people who need rides with a shorter lead time if possible, so it doesn't hurt to call and ask. If you need transport give them a call at 509.413.7986. Please share your experiences with the Trail of the Coeur d'Alenes Riders Facebook group.

Captain Lou's Bicycle Shuttle Service provides both car and boat shuttles for people and cycles. Lou can pick up/deliver to Trail of CdA trailheads, Route of the Hiawatha, Coeur d'Alene, and Spokane International Airport. Capacity on boat shuttles is six, but it could be less, depending on the type of equipment you have. Lou is based near Harrison and prefers not to serve the west side of the lake. Call or text 208.818.2254 to discuss your options.

Low Cost Transit & Trail Strategy

A combination of public transportation and dedicated trails can get you from Spokane to the Trail of the Coeur d'Alenes. One option is to catch Spokane Transit Authority bus #60 from Spokane Airport to the Bus Plaza, downtown Spokane, then cycle to Coeur d'Alene on bike trails. (Helmets are required in Spokane.) From the Bus Plaza, ride east one block on Riverside, and four blocks north on Howard. Enter Riverfront Park and look for the Spokane Centennial Trail markings on the ground next to the carousel. Ride this paved and mostly flat trail east about 38 miles to downtown Coeur d'Alene, Idaho.

If you would rather bus more than pedal through the Spokane Metro Area, board the #174 Liberty Lake Express at the Bus Plaza to the end of the line (16 miles) at Liberty Lake. From there, you can pick up the Spokane Centennial Trail at Harvard Trailhead, an easy 1.3 miles north on Harvard Rd. The Idaho state line is five miles east, and the trail continues to Coeur d'Alene as the North Idaho Centennial Trail.

Catch a free CityLink bus at Riverstone, before downtown Coeur d'Alene. It's about a three-hour ride from the Spokane Bus Plaza to Riverstone. Buses leave Riverstone for the **Coeur d'Alene Casino** near Worley, Idaho, every 85 minutes. From there, a Rural Route bus will drop you off right at the Plummer Trailhead. After a long day of riding trails and buses, rest up at the casino and get a fresh start to Plummer in the morning. CityLink buses carry from two to four cycles on a first-come-first-served basis, so be sure to arrive early. See both STA and CityLink Web sites for schedules and instructions on how to ride the bus with a cycle.

What About Trailways & Greyhound?

Northwest Trailways no longer stops in Plummer. **Greyhound** runs east west on I-90, and it's possible to travel round-trip between Spokane and Kellogg for about $60. The problem is, bikes have to be transported as baggage "packed in wood, canvas, or other substantial container." If the total dimensions exceed 62 inches, it costs $30 more. Even so, your bike might not make it if there isn't room in the baggage compartment. Overall, it is not cycle-friendly. Luckily, if you take the bus, there are two bike shops in Kellogg to take care of your rental requirements.

Hn'ya'(pqi'nn Trailhead (Gathering Place)

DRIVING DIRECTIONS: From I-90 take Hwy 95 (Sandpoint/Moscow exit) south 31 miles to Plummer. Turn right on Anne Antelope Rd. to trailhead parking.

TRAILHEAD AMENITIES: Restroom/Accessible (seasonal), Water, Picnic Area, Trail Info, 80 Park ing Spaces/5 ADA. Please park RVs in the west section of the parking area. CityLink Bus Stop. (Food, Lodging, Swimming, Shopping, Showers, Post Office nearby). **Next Stop: 2.4 miles**

Plummer, Idaho ELEVATION: 2,767 FT.

The City of Plummer, pop. 1,017, is the headquarters of the Coeur d'Alene Tribe. The trailhead is part of the Coeur d'Alene Tribe's *Hoy ch'ulte'lqu'lmkhw* **Veteran's Memorial Park**. The name denotes the Coeur d'Alene's interpretation of what it means to return back home after being at war. Fifteen miles of the trail traverse the Coeur d'Alene reservation and the tribe manages this portion. Trailheads on the reservation are named in the Coeur d'Alene language, and you will see historical markers that commemorate places and events significant to the tribe. *(See Pronunciation Key, page 19)*

Hoy ch'ulte'lqu'lmkhw Veteran's Memorial Park, Plummer, Idaho.

Plummer, Idaho

South, across the field from the trailhead, you can see the modern Coeur d'Alene Tribal **Wellness Center**. The public is welcome on a drop-in basis to enjoy the large **pool, spa, steam room**, and **exercise equipment**. Cost is $5 for adults and $2 for children 6 to 18. Showers only are $2. Summer hours are 5:30 a.m. to 7 p.m. weekdays, Sat. from 8 a.m. to 2 p.m. and Sun 11 a.m. to 6 p.m. Call 208.686.9355 for seasonal hours and pool hours. To avoid riding on Hwy. 95, exit on the west side of the trail parking area, head south, then turn left on "A" Street.

The Warpath gift shop borders Hwy. 95 just past the Wellness Center. It's the only place along the trails to get **gifts** with a Native American theme. The collection includes moccasins, sandals, Pendleton jackets, sweat shirts, music by tribal musicians, CDs, Indian jewelry, beads, leather, and other regalia supplies. **Plummer Hardware** is on the south side of the building. They have a small section of camping supplies and a few emergency **bike parts**, such as tubes and locks.

The **Gateway Café** is across the street on the corner of Hwy. 95 and "A" Street. This is a good place for a home-style meal in a friendly atmosphere. It's where the locals go for a hearty breakfast, lunch, or dinner. Omelettes, huckleberry pancakes, wraps, homemade soups, a salad bar, burgers, and sandwiches are a few items on the menu. Desserts include huckleberry specialties, such as ice cream, cheesecake, and home baked pies. They will gladly pack a sack lunch for you to enjoy along the trail.

Plummer, Idaho

Benewah Market is a tribally-owned full service grocery store next to Highway 95 and a block south of the Gateway Café. You will find a **Market Bistro**, **bakery**, fresh fruits and vegetables, fresh meat cut on

site, and any other groceries you may want to stock up on for the trail. This is also a place to get **bottled water**, energy bars, and any last minute needs.

The bakery proudly features a treat you won't find elsewhere for miles around: freshly prepared **donuts** fried in-house daily. The deli offers **breakfast biscuits**, burritos, fried chicken, fresh salads, and **sub sandwiches** made your way on bread baked in the store. Other services include **Western Union**, money orders, **ATM**, DVD rentals, and phone cards. **The CityLink bus** stops right out front. Inquire at the courtesy desk for departure times.

The Ace hardware store has a **small bicycle section** and most items found at an Ace hardware store, such as housewares and some **camping accessories.** They also sell fishing and hunting supplies. There are no more stores along the trail until Harrison, so stock up in Plummer.

Plummer, Idaho

Point of Interest: The Coeur d'Alene Tribe's aboriginal territory covered more than four million acres, from meadows west of here to the mountains in the east. Lake Coeur d'Alene was the crown jewel central to tribal society. In the late 1880s news of gold, silver, and vast stands of timber caused a stampede of strangers to the area. Soon, those who had lived here since time immemorial were considered to be in the way of progress. As pressures of encroachment mounted, priests at the Old Mission convinced some tribal leaders that a reservation with clear boundaries would be the tribe's best hope for survival. A reservation was established for exclusive tribal use, but in 1909, the US government reniged on its agreement and threw the reservation open to homesteaders. This resulted in cultural upheaval and economic hardship for tribal families, and a "checkerboard" pattern of land ownership and legal jurisdictional confusion that still causes consternation to this day. Despite the problems that come with being colonized, the Coeur d'Alene tribe has risen to prominence in the region. They are among north Idaho's top employers, and share their success through generous contributions to education, health care, and public transportation that benefit people both on and off the reservation.

COEUR D'ALENE LANGUAGE PRONUNCIATION KEY

hn'ya'(pqi'nn	Gathering Place
hn-tsaq-aq-n	Stopping Place
hn-pet-pt-qwe'n	Place for Racing
hn-dar-ep	Canoe Landing
sqwe'-mu'-lmkhw	A Familiar Place

In general, the hyphens indicate the separation of significant parts (prefixes, verb roots, suffixes), but they also fit pretty neatly into syllable breaks. The stressed syllable has the vowel bolded.

The *hn-* prefix means 'place,' and is pronounced something like (Atilla the) hun, or hin(ge), or hen(-house), but without much of a vowel in the middle. It's closer to a schwa.

In the way that the tribe chooses to represent these sounds, there is no schwa (upside down 'e'), but you can probably imagine what it sounds like by noticing that it belongs before *n, m, r, l*, as in the last syllable of '*button, item, actor, level.*'

Each '*e*' above sounds like the vowel in *pet, bet, get, bed*, etc. All of the '*a*' sounds rhyme with *saw, wad, odd, pod*, etc. The '*i* ' is like a long-e, '*mean, feed, fiend, army, machine.*'

Pronunciation key courtesy of the Coeur d'Alene Tribe Language Program

Plummer, Idaho

The **post office** is around the corner from Benewah Market on Hwy. 95. Go south another block to the junction with State Route 5 (SR-5) for the **Hiway Motel,** Plummer's only lodging option. If you plan to fish along the trail, you can get a **license** there.

Rising Star Espresso stand, one more block south on Hwy. 95, opens early daily. They serve hot and cold **coffee drinks,** teas, granitas, and chai. They have almond milk and soy milk options, and fresh fruit smoothies. The jalapeno bagel with cream cheese is a local favorite. The baristas make specialty drinks by request, and they give out Trail of the Coeur d'Alenes **maps** when available.

Ride east on "D" Street two blocks to 8th Street, to the **Plummer Public Library.** They open Mon. through Wed., 10 a.m. to 6 p.m., Thurs. 2 to 6 p.m. and Sat. 10 a.m. to 2 p.m. Public access computers are available for 30 minutes at a time on a drop-in basis, or longer when reserved.

Point of Interest: This is the vicinithy of Plummer's original settlement, of which barely anything remains. When homesteaders arrived in 1910, they found an old growth Ponderosa pine forest so thick and tall the sun barely shone through. The trees were cut down by hand to make room for tent sites and the first Old West style buildings. Tree removal was a major occupation in those early days and the wealth of timber in the area kept at least three sawmills operating day and night.

Turn left on 8th, at the Library to find **AVUBAH:** A Very Unique Boutique and Antique House, in the brightly painted old house a half block north. Cyclists are welcome to picnic in the shady yard.

Plummer, Idaho

Point of Interest: The dilapidated white building across from AVUBAH is the old City Market, one of the few remaining relics of what was once a bustling business district with wooden sidewalks that provided some respite from the muddy streets.

Bobbi's famous rez bar, is next to AVUBAH. "Famous" for its part in Sherman Alexie's Native American classic, *Smoke Signals*. Many locals acted as extras in the film. People drop in just to see the peavys, chokers, and saws on the walls, that are reminders of the area's logging heritage. An avid supporter of live music, especially the blues, Bobbi's hosts bands on selected weekends. Upcoming acts are posted at facebook.com/Bobbis.Bar. Pizzas, egg rolls, and assorted boxed dinners are available daily until 1 a.m. at this full-service lounge.

Point of Interest: Bobbi's is one of the oldest remaining buildings in town. It got its start as Frank McCaslin's Plummer Mercantile in 1914. Through the years it also served as the American Legion Hall, a supper club called the Pink Sarang, and the Main Street Mill bar. It is the site of the town's first water well, which was drilled out back by the building's original owner. The townspeople flocked here with jugs and buckets to collect fresh water for their daily needs. Before that, heavy buckets had to be carried from springs near Plummer Butte or Plummer Creek. Hobos and other itinerants travelling through by railroad would often be hired to haul water for a few cents.

When you are ready to start your journey, proceed from the trailhead through the tunnel and ride along the outskirts of Plummer for about a mile, before being treated to a scenic six-mile descent through Plummer Canyon. The trail follows an old Indian footpath that was part of an ancient network that led to the Rocky Mountains and beyond. Bear sightings are fairly common along this stretch of the trail.

Hn-tsaq-aq-n Scenic Wayside (Stopping Place) Trail Miles: 2.7

WHERE AM I?
Overlooking Plummer Creek on the Coeur d'Alene Indian Reservation.

REST AREA AMENITIES: Restroom/Accessible, Picnic Table, Interpretive Sign.
Next Stop: 1.8 miles

Hn-pet-pt-qwe'n Scenic Wayside (Place for Racing)
Trail Miles: 4.5

WHERE AM I?
Plummer Canyon on the Coeur d'Alene Indian Reservation.

REST AREA AMENITIES: Restroom/Accessible, Picnic Table, Interpretive Sign.
Next Stop: 1.7 miles

Trail Miles: 6.2 ## Indian Cliffs Trailhead

DRIVING DIRECTIONS: From I-90 take HWY 95 south 32 miles to SR-5. Head east six miles and turn left on Chatcolet Rd. Stop at the office for a parking permit. Indian Cliffs Trailhead is 1.2 miles on the left, but the small parking area there is reserved for Indian Cliffs hikers. Trail parking is 1.3 miles ahead at Chatcolet Trailhead.

TRAILHEAD AMENITIES: Interpretive Sign, Hiking Trails, (Restroom/Accessible, Water, Picnic Area, Lodging, Camping, Swimming, Rentals, Showers nearby)

Deer in Heyburn State Park

Next Stop: 1.3 miles

ELEVATION: 2,128 FT. **Heyburn State Park/Heyburn Park**

(The State of Idaho refers to this area as Heyburn State Park. The Coeur d'Alene Tribe calls it Heyburn Park. Both references are used within the co-managed area).

Heyburn is Idaho's oldest state park. It has 26 miles of **trails** for hikers, mountain bikers, and horseback riders. The hiking trail at Indian Cliffs Trailhead is about three miles, moderate to steep. Watch for wildlife as the trail ascends through scenic stands of pine, fir, cedar, hemlock, and Pacific yew. From the top you can get a good view of the St. Joe River and lakes that converge in the park for your boating, fishing, and swimming pleasure. An easy to moderate one-mile CCC Nature Trail intersects Indian Cliffs Trail near the trailhead.

For **Park headquarters** and Hawley's Landing **campground**, take Chatcolet Rd. south (right) for 1.2 miles. There is a **restroom** at the

Plummer Marsh area along the way. Pay fees, get **visitor information**, trail maps, and nature guides at headquarters.

Overnight accommodations in the park include **tent and RV camping**, rustic **cabins**, and two-bedroom **cottages** that sleep up to eight people. Cabins and cottages are available year round and there is a three-night minimum stay. Lodgings in the park are in high demand, especially during summer, so make reservations early online at

Wildlife viewing shed at Plummer Marsh, Heyburn Park

parksandrecreation.idaho.gov, or call. 888.922.6743.

Heyburn State Park/Heyburn Park

Hawley's Landing campground next to park headquarters has **free interpretive programs** all summer, such as crafts, nature walks, and guided **canoe trips**. There are free showers here for campers. Day visitors can **shower for $3**.

If you are riding the entire Bitterroot Loop in a counterclockwise direction, the 13-mile highway portion to St. Maries starts at the park entrance. The route is a two-lane rural commuter route with scant shoulders and quite a bit of uphill pedaling. Courtesy shuttles between here and St. Maries are offered to guests who stay at the **Pines Motel** or **Fort Hemenway Manor**. This guidebook takes the clockwise route, so we'll be visiting St. Maries later, on page 99.

As you continue toward Chatcolet Trailhead from Indian Cliffs, you can see the Osprey and Heron **camping cabins** tucked into the trees to your left .2 mile down the trail. They have power, but water and vault toilet are outside. Cabins include a microwave and sleep 3 (with bunk). Bring your own bedding. Watch for the path on the right. It leads to Plummer Point, with a nice secluded **picnic** shelter and **swimming** beach. There is a **water fountain** as well.

Chatcolet Trailhead
Trail Miles: 7.5

DRIVING DIRECTIONS: From I-90 take HWY 95 south 32 miles to SR-5. Head east six miles and turn left at the park entrance onto Chatcolet Rd. Stop at the office for a parking permit, $5/day MVEF parking fee. Drive 2.5 miles north. Bear right at the fork and go downhill toward the large parking area next to the lake.

Chacolet Bridge in Heyburn Park

TRAILHEAD AMENITIES: Public Restroom/ Accessible, Water (seaonal). Picnic Area, Trail Info, Swimming. 100 Parking Spaces/none ADA marked. Large unpaved parking lot with plenty of room for RVs. (Lodging, Camping, Hiking nearby). Camping is only allowed in designated campgrounds, but vehicles may be left at the trailhead for an additional $5.30 per night while you ride the trails. Inquire at headquarters. **Next Stop: 2.5 miles.**

Heyburn State Park/Heyburn Park

The park's **tent campground** is up the hill behind the Chatcolet day use **picnic area**. Cycles can be walked to the campground from the Trail of the Coeur d'Alenes on a grassy trail between the parking area and Chatcolet bridge. Otherwise it's a steep half-mile climb by road from the parking lot. In that case, head uphill, bear right through the fork and continue past the **Chatcolet Rental Cabin** to the tent area. There is a host at the campground during summer. You can also check yourself in at the sign, but advance reservations are highly recommended via reserveamerica.com. **Firewood** is available for purchase.

Point of Interest: Hike along a portion of the **historic Mullan Road** from the interpretive sign at the tent campground. Capt. John Mullan and his crew were here in 1859 chopping and hacking a 624-mile swath from Walla Walla, Washington, to the Missouri River. They constructed a "corduroy" log bridge from the shore to the St. Joe River. This branch of the Mullan road was later abandoned for a drier route to the north—the present day I-90. But many determined gold seekers, loggers, and backwoods entrepreneurs continued to use this old Mullan trail to access the St. Joe River country to the east.

Chatcolet Lake, Hidden Lake, Round Lake, and the southern end of Lake Coeur d'Alene, all lie within the park. Flooding caused by the Post Falls Dam makes them look like one big lake. Trees that appear to be growing out of the water are actually the banks of the St. Joe River, which is also submerged because of the dam.

More than fifty osprey pairs nest in this area. If you see a huge nest perched on top of Chatcolet Bridge, it most likely belongs to an osprey.

Ask at park headquarters for a list of birds who find habitat here.

Chatcolet Bridge was originally designed to swing open for steamboats cruising the St. Joe River. It was retrofitted to become one of the trail's most striking features. The stair step design makes the ascent easier, and the descent fun.

family nudist resort

A unique connecting trip and safe alternative for women travelers is 3.5 miles from Chatcolet Trailhead at the gated **Sun Meadow Family Nudist Resort**. Getting there requires a steep 1.4-mile climb from Chatcolet Trailhead, so cycling guests should inquire about a **courtesy shuttle** from the trailhead when making reservations.

The resort includes a main lodge with **large indoor pool, fitness center**, rec-room, **library**, free wireless **Internet**, and **hotel rooms** with private bathrooms. The lodge has a multipurpose hall with big screen movies, dancing, and **musical performances** by national acts. Nutritious **home cooked meals** are served daily and the chef is happy to accommodate special dietary needs. Inquire about morning **yoga**, pool exercises, and **massages**.

The grounds include 47 full-service **RV sites, cabin**, shady **tent area, outdoor pool, hot tub**, playground, **bocce** court, volleyball court, pond, and **hiking** trails. There is a pet-friendly RV to rent. Advance lodging reservations are recommended but not required. Are you new to social nudism? Call the friendly staff with any questions or concerns.

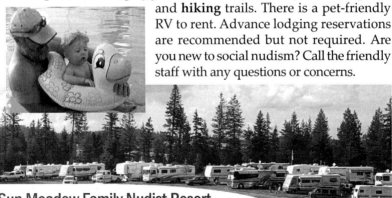

Sun Meadow Family Nudist Resort
sunmeadow.org   30400 S. Sunray Trail, Worley, Idaho 83876   **208.686.8686**

Experience another unique Connecting Trip at the **H2H Bison Ranch**, where buffalo roam on 35 forested acres. The camp is just 3.5 miles west of Chatcolet Trailhead and offers full service **RV sites,** a cozy **tipi,** and **camping cabins** that have mini-fridge, coffee pot, and Wifi, but running water and toilet are outside. People traveling light by cycle may arrange for bedding to be supplied in the cabins. The hot outdoor shower is a favorite feature. Guests are free to use the **barbecue** and "pit kitchen," complete with modern appliances. Request groceries to be waiting when you arrive so you don't have to worry about packing food. Relax around the **bonfire**, where owners Buzz and Melissa will share **stories** about the fascinating bison. It's a steep climb from Chatcolet Trailhead, so when making reservations, inquire about a **courtesy shuttle** for two or more guests.

h2hbisonranch.com
208.755.6102
h2hbisonranch@gmail.com

H2H
BISON RANCH
30585 S. Ditmore Rd,
Worley, Id 83876

Hn-dar-ep Scenic Wayside (Canoe Landing) Trail Miles: 10

WHERE AM I?
The southeastern bank of Lake Coeur d'Alene within the Coeur d'Alene Indian Reservation.

REST AREA AMENITIES:
Restroom/Accessible, Picnic Table, Interpretive Sign.
Next Stop: 2.1 miles

Sqwe'-mu'-lmkhw Scenic Wayside (A Familiar Place)
Trail Miles: 12.1

WHERE AM I?
The southeastern bank of Lake Coeur d'Alene within the Coeur d'Alene Indian Reservation.

REST AREA AMENITIES: Restroom/ Accessible, Picnic Table, Interpretive Sign.
Next Stop: 2.9 miles

Point of Interest: When the Coeur d'Alene Tribe's lands were thrown open to settlers, 160-acres of white pine sold for up to $15,000. Consequently, much of the reservation land was "homesteaded" with the express intention of selling it to lumber companies. Many logs from the St. Joe River country were floated past here to be processed at mills that crowded the Harrison waterfront.

Steamboat Landing Scenic Wayside Trail Miles: 15

WHERE AM I?
The southeastern bank of Lake Coeur d'Alene, within Harrison city limits, in Kootenai County.

REST AREA AMENITIES:
Interpretive Sign.
Next Stop: .3 mile

Looking south from the trail on the seven-mile portion that hugs Lake Coeur d'Alene

Trail Miles: 15.3   ## Harrison Marina Trailhead

DRIVING DIRECTIONS: Take I-90 Wolf Lodge Bay/Harrison Exit #22 south 28 miles on the Lake Coeur d'Alene Scenic Byway (Hwy. 97). Turn right on the south end of Harrison's city park, go down the hill one block and turn left. Please park at the "trail parking" signs. The lower lot on the lake level is for marina customers and campers. However, if handicapped, you may use the ADA spot at the bottom of the hill by the public beach.

TRAILHEAD AMENITIES: Restroom/ Accessible, Picnic Area, Trail Information, Camping, Swimming, (Water, Food, Lodging, Shopping, Museum, Rentals, Laundry, Post Office nearby). **Next Stop: 1.3 miles**

The quaint resort town of Harrison is a favorite stop on the lake for cyclists, campers, and boaters.

ELEVATION: 2,150 FT.   ## Harrison, Idaho

Many cyclists choose picturesque Harrison, Idaho, (pop. 210) as a base from which to explore the trail. It's where the lake, trail, and visitor services converge. There is **RV and tent camping** next to the trailhead on the lake. Go for a dip at the sandy **public beach** along the trail. The vault **toilet** across from the beach is open year round. Day visitors may use the coin-operated **shower** in the campground, where you can get a quick warm shower for six quarters. One of three popular marinas on the south lake is in Harrison, so boaters flock here for food, spirits, and dancing on hot summer nights. The city campground is centrally located in the midst of the action so don't expect it to be a quiet spot on weekend evenings. See **southlakecda.com** for listings of **live music acts**, lodging links, and events around south Lake Coeur d'Alene.

The Trail of the Coeur d'Alenes (lower left) goes by the city beach and marina

Harrison, Idaho *"Where the Trail Meets the Lake"*

Enter to Win an Overnight Getaway in Harrison
Details at harrisonidaho.org

Live Music in the Park
Saturdays in Summer

Pig in the Park
Harrison Craft & Trade Fair
Saturday, June 13, 2015
Harrison City Park

4th of July
Fireworks on the Lake
Downtown Harrison

Haul Ass to Harrison
Annual Classic Car Show
Plus Classical Glass Boat Show 'n Shine
September 12, 2015
Harrison City Park and Waterfront

Oktoberfest
Saturday, October 3, 2015
Harrison City Park

Winterfest
Saturday, December 5, 2015
Downtown Harrison

IDAHO
www.visitidaho.org

VisitNorthIdaho.com

Harrison
Chamber of Commerce
www.harrisonidaho.org

Harrison, Idaho

Harrison is all about fun on the water and **Harrison Pontoons & Rentals** specializes in getting you there with top-of-the-line equipment **rentals**. Up to sixteen people can enjoy the 24-foot Performance JC Tritoons, which, unlike most **pontoon boats**, go

Harrison Pontoons & Rentals offers a variety of boats, water toys, and package deals with vacation rentals on the lake.

fast enough to pull **skiis and tubes**. Another option is the Sea-Doo Speedster. It's a cross be tween a jet ski and jet boat and pulls tubes and skis. You can also rent a Bass Tracker or smaller aluminum **fishing boat** from this local family-owned business. The Reinhardt family also offers comfy **vacation homes** in the area, so check out the package deals online at harrison pontoons.com, or call 208.696.1770.

Famous **One Shot Charlie's** café and bar is up the hill from the trailhead in the historic brick building that once housed the International Order of Odd Fellows. Famous because just about anywhere you go in the Inland Northwest, you run into folks who have partied at One Shots. During summer, the bar and cafe' are open seven days a week for lunch and dinner. The bar features fun creative cocktails and rotating craft and domestic draft handles. The café serves pizza, sandwiches, burgers, fresh salads and lasagna. Outdoor seating overlooks the park and marina. **Live music** and special theme parties happen year round and are posted on One Shot Charlie's facebook page.

The Tin Cup is up the hill on the corner of the building's second level. They serve organic free trade coffee drinks and a limited breakfast selec-

Harrison, Idaho

tion of quiche, baked goods, oatmeal, fresh fruit, and yogurt. Open five days a week, between 7 a.m. and 2 p.m. in summer, they are closed Thursday and Friday. The Tin Cup also accepts orders for "take-n-bake" quiches, pot pies, and fruit pies. Ask what they have on hand or what they're willing to make on custom order. 208.689.3088. Closed in winter, they reopen for the season in April.

Also, on the second level find **O'Susanna's Design Studio**, a salon and gallery, where in addition to hair styling services, Susan carries beach dresses, and sells jewelry and glass art creations she makes. The **Denise Oliver Gallery** above One Shot Charlie's is a favorite stop for art lovers. Owners Denise and Terry Oliver retired in 2014. The gallery will continue to operate under new management, open May through end of September. As of this writing, local artisanal soap makers are planning to open **Grubby Girls Soap** where they will showcase their homemade soaps in the space that previously housed The Glass Crane gift shop next to the gallery.

Gig's Landing, a half block south, features fresh seafood, pasta dishes, hand cut fries and steaks, seasonal salads, sandwiches, and housemade sauces with quality ingredients. Enjoy classic cocktails, Northwest wines, and craft drafts on the deck while watching a spectacular Harrison sunset over the lake.

Visitors line up for ice cream at The Creamery next to Gig's Landing

Most buildings downtown are on the National Register of Historic Places. The **Crane House Museum** across the street, is the city's oldest building. See Harrison's artifacts there and ponder its glory days as the former largest city in Kootenai County. Browse the old city jail, model steamboats, antique furnishings, and logging and milling machinery. The museum has old photos, books, and a collection of **local oral histories** on CD for sale. Ask for a free map of the self-guided historical building tour. The volunteer-run museum opens weekends from Memorial to Labor Day, noon until 4 p.m. Admission is free, but donations are appreciated.

Harrison City Park, in the heart of downtown, is flocked by big shade trees and beautiful flowers. It overlooks the trailhead and lake, and many cyclists can be found resting here. There is free live music Saturday afternoons during summer. **Restrooms** with flush toilets are open seasonally.

Point of Interest: Harrison had 1,200 residents and a lively business district until 1917, when a fire destroyed much of the town, including 11 businesses that stood where the park is now. The rubble remained until 1953, when members of the Old Timer's Picnic group cleaned it up for their annual gathering. Now most community events are centered in the park.

The **public library** (with Wifi) is across from the park. Look for the outdoor Grange Market on Saturdays, starting 10 a.m., in the pocket park next to the library. The **post office** is also on this block.

Harrison Trading Post, on the corner is a combination grocery store, deli, bakery, and liquor store. They have coffee, breakfast sandwiches, and fresh baked pastries in the morning. The deli section has sandwiches to order and prepared salads. You can also find an **ATM** and Harrison area souvenirs here. The next food and water are 25-miles away at Cataldo, so stock up before leaving Harrison.

Pedal Pushers Bike Shop, across from the market, is a full service **bike rental, retail, and repair shop**, and authorized **Trek** dealer. They provide expert cycle repairs to get you on the trail in a hurry. The rental bike selection includes comfort bikes, tandems, recumbents, children's bikes and trailers. Order an **espresso** and browse the riding gear, or enjoy your drink on the porch.

Harrison, Idaho

Step into **Sheppard Fruit Wines'** **tasting room** next door to sample delicious wines crafted on nearby Harrison Flats. Owners Julie and Jim Sheppard pick and buy much of the fruit for their wines locally. The crush for 2015 is: cranberry, huckleberry, raspberry, elderberry, pear, and rhubarb. Tasting costs $4, which is credited to your purchase. Readers of this trail guide are offered an additional **5% off deal** on their purchase when mentioning the book, so don't be shy and take advantage of this little perk. The tasting room is open noon to 5 p.m. starting late spring through summer. They post updates about the status of their wines and other news on Facebook.

The Bird's Nest opened in the brick Grant Building across the street in 2013, and instantly became a popular stop for gift shopping. It features lodge and cabin décor, and garden art that conveys the Northwest lifestyle. Souvenirs with lake and **cycle themes**, and moose, bear, deer, birds, and other outdoor designs, decorate cups, shirts, bags, treats, and customized signs. Find quality scarves, jewelry, skin care products, comical greeting cards, retro **postcards** and more here. The Bird's nest is open daily July through mid-October, with seasonal hours in autumn and spring. In winter, Shelly may open by special request if she's around, so give her a call.

Harrison, Idaho

The Company Store in the historic Grant Building is filled with antique, vintage and upcycled wares, and architectural salvage. The building originally served as a general store with a meeting hall upstairs for Harrison's Freemasons.

Browsing the Company Store has become a popular visitors' past time as the wares spark conversations about memories and stories of bygone times. The constantly revolving collection includes items from historic Harrison, the Silver Valley, Spokane, and Seattle, including both antique and newly handcrafted furniture, gently used boutique clothing, art, tools, glass, Pyrex, vinyl, vintage fixtures, trinkets, and old books that people carry out by the armload. Some shoppers haul their treasures home by boat. (Cyclists may want to inquire about shipping). The store is open daily in summer from about 10 a.m. to 6 p.m., and sometimes later. In fall and winter, hours are generally Thursday through Sunday, noon to 5 p.m. If you are visiting Harrison during the slow season, somebody is usually around to come and open the doors. Make arrangements by calling Paul Hoskinson, 208-699-2228 or email paul@companystore.biz.

The **Laundromat** on the lower level was closed after being vandalized last year, but it will be in service again for the 2015 cycle season.

Harrison, Idaho

Go one block northeast to **Lakeview Lodge**, where every unit has a private balcony and unobstructed lake view. The rooms are tastefully decorated in cabin style, each with unique touches. They all have air conditioning, free **Internet**, coffee makers, refrigerators, and microwaves. The larger suites upstairs have **kitchenettes** stocked with everything required for an extended stay; just bring the food. Guests may also use the barbecue. The lodge is a favorite among cyclists, who may be found relaxing at a table on the patio, sipping a glass of their favorite beverage and sharing trail adventures with other riders. Lock cycles to the railing, or ask for secure bicycle storage. The public beach, park, restaurants, bars and trail are all within short walking distance of the lodge. Guests may park vehicles here free while continuing to explore the local trails. Lakeview Lodge is open all year. They don't use an online booking system, so call for reservations.

Point of Interest: During the 1917 fire, Harrison's residents tried to save their belongings by carrying them out into the streets. One item that survived is a piano that later found a home in the basement of the Baptist church across the street. The veneer is falling off on one side but it still sounds fine.

CORSKIE HOUSE B&B, (previously the Wild Boar Inn), is next door to the motel. Another popular stopover for cyclists, the house was built by Idaho's first known pharmacist after the 1917 fire destroyed his home. The immaculate inn over-

Harrison, Idaho

looks the lake and has four bedrooms, private baths, **Wifi**, and a den with **pool table**. Relax on the back porch and enjoy the lake view. There is secure cycle storage on site and owner, Russ Wilbur, serves a **hearty breakfast** to get you on the trail in the morning.

For the **Osprey Inn Bed & Breakfast**, ride two blocks northeast on Hwy 97. This boutique B&B in a historical building has five vintage hotel rooms decorated with antiques. Each has a private bath with shower. There is free Wifi and a common room to watch TV and movies. New owners, Larry and Sherry, share their love of breakfast by offering three options: a continental breakfast for early birds, a three-course meal at 9 a.m., or a boxed breakfast to take on the go. There is secure storage for cycles. See details at ospreyinnbnb.com. 208.689.9502.

Wildlife Area Day Ride

Look for birds and wildlife along a mostly flat back road loop ride out of Harrison around Thompson Lake. Start by taking the Trail of the Coeur d'Alenes along the river to Springston Trailhead and cross over the wooden plank bridge. Turn right on paved Blue Lake Rd. and go 1.5-miles to the intersection. Follow the road left around the lake. It turns to dirt after .3-mile. See the Thompson Lake cutoff 1.3 miles later. The trail on the left leads to a free primitive Idaho Fish & Game camping and swimming area along the lakeshore. See the wildlife viewing blind a mile later. After another 1.2-miles the road comes out on Hwy. 97. Ride the highway for .5 mile and turn left onto Blue Lake Rd. It's 1.8 miles back to the bridge at Springston Trailhead. Return to Harrison on the trail, or for a more challenging ride, take the 3.5-mile trip around Anderson Lake Rd. There are more swimming and free primitive camping areas within a mile of the bridge, after which there is a climb for about 1.5 miles. Anderson Lake Rd. comes out on Hwy. 97, and it's .9 mile back to Harrison from there.

Thompson Lake, one of the chain lakes along the Coeur d'Alene River

Point of Interest: Anderson and Thompson Lakes are part of the chain lakes and the 22-mile long Coeur D'Alene River Wildlife Management Area. Canada Goose, Yellow Warbler, Black Tern, Violet-green Swallow; and Pied-billed, Red-necked, and Horned Grebe find habitat here. Look for Tundra Swans along Blue Lake and keep an eye out for nesting eagles. Nesting osprey build huge nests on the utility poles.

Anderson Lake Scenic Wayside   Trail Miles: 16.6

WHERE AM I?
The south side of the Coeur d'Alene River, Kootenai County.

REST AREA AMENITIES: Picnic Table, Interpretive Sign.
Next Stop: 1.8 miles

Springston Trailhead   Trail Miles: 18.4

Springston Bridge over the Coeur d'Alene River

DRIVING DIRECTIONS: Take I-90 to Wolf Lodge Bay/Harrison Exit #22 and drive south 26 miles along (Hwy 97), Lake Coeur d'Alene Scenic Byway. Turn left onto Blue Lake Rd. before the bridge and drive 1.8 miles. Trailhead is over the wooden plank bridge.

TRAILHEAD AMENITIES: Restroom/ Accessible, Picnic Table, Trail Info, 13 Parking Spaces/1 ADA.
Next Stop: 1.2 miles

Point of Interest: Springston became a stop on the Oregon Washington Railway and Navigation line and served as a shipping point for lumber. People from Thompson Lake, Blue Lake, Harrison Flats, Medimont, and Rose Lake shopped at the store here, which was close to where the restrooms are now. The remains of the tugboat *Golden Star* lie near the bridge. By taking the dirt road opposite the bridge (southeast) you can access several undeveloped swimming areas at pullouts along a mile-long stretch of Anderson Lake.

Cottonwood Scenic Wayside   Trail Miles: 19.6

WHERE AM I?
The south bank of the Coeur d'Alene River in Kootenai County. Thompson Lake is to the north.

REST AREA AMENITIES: Picnic Table, Interpretive Sign.
Next Stop: 1.1 miles

Trail Miles: 20.7   ## Gray's Meadow Scenic Wayside

WHERE AM I?
The south bank of the Coeur d'Alene River in Kootenai County.

REST AREA AMENITIES: Picnic Table, Interpretive Sign.
Next Stop: 3.5 miles

Trail Miles: 24.2   ## Cave Lake Scenic Wayside

WHERE AM I?
The south bank of the Coeur d'Alene River between Swan Lake and Cave Lake in Kootenai County.

REST AREA AMENITIES: Restroom/ Accessible, Picnic Table, Interpretive Sign. **Next Stop: 1.6 miles**

Trail Miles: 25.8   # Medimont Trailhead

Medimont Trailhead

DRIVING DIRECTIONS: Take I-90 to the Rose Lake Exit #34. Travel south on the White Pine Scenic Byway (SR-3) for 12.2 miles to the Medimont turnoff. Turn right and drive 1.5 miles to the trailhead.

TRAILHEAD AMENITIES: Restroom/Accessible, Picnic Area, Trail Info, 12 Parking Spaces/1 ADA. **Next Stop: 3.8 miles**

Point of Interest: The name Medimont was coined from "Medicine Mountain," because the local Indians traditionally gathered cascara here. The town was settled in the 1890s in anticipation of great mineral wealth in the nearby mountains.

Trail Miles: 29.6   ## Lane Scenic Wayside

WHERE AM I?
Between the south bank of the Coeur d'Alene River and SR-3 in Kootenai County.

REST AREA AMENITIES: Restroom/ Accessible, Picnic Table, Interpretive Sign.
Next Stop: 1.6 miles

Point of Interest: Melissa Anderson Moe was the first white woman to live in these parts, and she birthed her daughter Ruby in a log cabin nearby. In the early days, she and her neighbors relied on the railroad to bring supplies. Before a station was built, the crew would blow the whistle, slow down, and toss the freight on the ground. Anyone expecting a package would walk along the tracks for a half mile or so, looking for their things. By 1910, Lane had a hotel and two large stores.

Black Rock Trailhead Trail Miles: 31.2

DRIVING DIRECTIONS: Take I-90 to the Rose Lake Exit #34 and travel south on SR-3 6.1 miles. Turn right after the bridge across the Coeur d'Alene River.

TRAILHEAD AMENITIES: Picnic Table, Interpretive Sign. 13 Parking Spaces, none marked ADA.
Next Stop: 2.3 miles

Bull Run Lake Trailhead Trail Miles 33.5

DRIVING DIRECTIONS: Take I-90 to Rose Lake Exit #34 and travel south on SR-3 3.2 miles to the community of Rose Lake where you will see a sign pointing to the trailhead. Turn left over the single-lane bridge, then right to the parking area.

TRAILHEAD AMENITIES: Restroom/ Accessible, Picnic Area, Trail Info, 10 Parking Spaces/1 ADA. **Next Stop: 1.4 miles**

Rose Lake, Idaho

Point of Interest: The settlement at Rose Lake sprang up around the Winton Lumber Co. mill along the railroad near Bull Run Trailhead. Some 900 people lived at Rose Lake until the Great Depression, when the mill shut down. There was a general store, ice cream parlor, barber, butcher, and boarding house for single men. The company built a large YMCA with tennis courts, bowling alley, and library. Silent movies accompanied by a pianist were shown weekly.

Watsons Rose Lake Resort is two miles north of Bull Run Trailhead near SR-3. The rustic resort has several lodging and camping options off the beaten path. Reservations are required. The **vacation rental** suite above a **historic tavern** sleeps eight, or can be rented by the room with shared bath and kitchen. Take SR-3 north for 1.6 miles then turn left on Watson Rd. The resort is .5 mile farther at the end of the road. They are not offering a shuttle at time of writing. Before the resort, you can turn off to a public **campground** where there is a **restroom**, **picnic area**, and boat launch on Rose Lake.

Rose Lake, Idaho

The view from the "glamping" cabin at Watson's Resort

Self-contained RVs and tents are welcome at Watson's grassy grounds that overlook the lake. There are also two **camping cabins**. Bedding is provided in the cabins, but running water and toilet facilities are outside. There is a bowl and pitcher, like back in the old days. Ask for the cabin with the luxurious bed and lake view. Both have mini-fridge, microwave, coffee maker, and TV with VHS movies that can be borrowed free. The second cabin sleeps up to four, but it's tight. Bring enough food to last until you get to the restaurant in Cataldo because the tavern, which serves pizza, is only open occasionally. Your only other breakfast/lunch option (not dinner) is to ride north two miles on SR-3 to the Rose Lake Restaurant or the quick stops. See watsonsroselake resort.com or call 208.691.0596 for reservations.

Trail Miles: 34.9   Cedar Grove Scenic Wayside

WHERE AM I?
The south bank of the Coeur d'Alene River in Kootenai County.

REST AREA AMENITIES: Picnic Table, Interpretive Sign.
Next Stop: 1.5 miles

Trail Miles: 36.4   Dudley Scenic Wayside

WHERE AM I?
The south bank of the Coeur d'Alene River in Kootenai County.

REST AREA AMENITIES: Picnic Table, Interpretive Sign.
Next Stop: 2.2 miles

Trail Miles: 38.6   River Bend Scenic Wayside

WHERE AM I?
The south bank of the Coeur d'Alene River in Kootenai County.

REST AREA AMENITIES: Restroom, Picnic Table, Interpretive Sign.
Next Stop: 1.5 mile

Trail Miles 40.1   Latour Creek Scenic Wayside

WHERE AM I?
The mouth of Latour Creek on the south bank of the Coeur d'Alene River in Kootenai County.

REST AREA AMENITIES: Picnic Table, Interpretive Sign.
Next Stop: 1.9 miles

Kahnderosa Campground, .2 mile before the Cataldo Trailhead, has lots of room for **RV camping** and **tenting** along the river.

Cataldo Trailhead

Trail Miles: 42

DRIVING DIRECTIONS: Take 1-90 to Exit #40. Off ramps from both sides of I-90 lead to Latour Creek Rd. Turn right and drive to the stop sign. The trailhead is on the left within .2 mile or less, depending on the ramp used.

TRAILHEAD AMENITIES: Portable Toilet (removed after the peak season), Picnic Area, Trail Info, 10 Parking Spaces/1 ADA. (Bottled Water, Food, Camping, Post Office nearby). **Next Stop: 1.6 miles**

Cataldo, Idaho   ELEVATION: 2,140 FT.

This is the unincorporated town of Cataldo, 27 miles east of Coeur d'Alene, on the border of Kootenai and Shoshone counties. The **post office** is adjacent to the trailhead.

You can have a **home cooked breakfast, lunch, or dinner** at the award winning **Mission Inn Café & Grill** across from the trailhead. Noted for **best chef, steak, wine and beer selection,** and **best server/ bar tender** in the Silver Valley. They offer a wide selection of breakfast dishes until noon. For lunch or dinner, choose from among the fresh salads, or create your own from the salad bar. There is a large array of burgers and sandwiches, homemade soups, chili, steaks, prawns, oysters, cod, and salmon. Pair your meal with beer or wine from the huge selection, or have a shake. **Healthy fish tacos** made with poached cod and topped with tasty mango salsa and Louie Sauce, are popular favorites that keep people coming back. Same with the **Pulled pork** sandwiches and **barbecue ribs,** made with Ann's signature barbecue sauces. (Purchase Anne's sauce to go by the pint or quart). Don't forget to leave room for pie.

Dine inside or under the beautiful trees outside. Free primitive camping is available. Catch up on your networking with the **free Wifi.** Local musicians join the open jam sessions on Thursday evenings. Better get some bottled **water** for the next leg of the journey.

Cataldo, Idaho

Point of Interest: These woods were filled with rugged and colorful characters with names like Terrible Tom Kitts, Chew the Rag Casey, Cruel Jim Holmes, Nellie the Bilk, and Gentle Doc Busby. They worked long hard hours for little pay. If they had a quirk, unusual talent, or braved a difficulty, word spread through homesteads and logging camps in the woods like wildfire. Jack Kerr rode logs like a cat. The Hunt brothers roped a bear that was after their lunch pails up Cedar Creek. Masamo, the cobbler, kept his long mustache out of the way by tucking it behind his ears. Beanery waitress, Olive Christman, entertained diners with her ability to lick her own ears. Old Man Heanecraft, a woodsman who lived up a draw out of Cataldo, got his hand caught in one of his traps and cut it off so he could walk to town for help. The hardy bunch of prospectors, settlers, and lumberjacks unwound at places like the Wayside Inn, where the Cataldo post office now stands.

This cabin of G.F Smith near Eagle City, was typical of homes all over the woods from Plummer to Mullan, c. 1890. Historic Wallace Preservation Society, Inc.

Coeur d'Alenes Old Mission, The state's oldest building, Cataldo, Idaho

The Coeur d'Alene's Old Mission State Park is on the site of a traditional Coeur d'Alene tribal village. This Connecting Trip provides enriching historical perspective and cultural understanding of the land you are cycling through. Idaho's oldest standing building, the Sacred Heart Mission, is here, along with a parish house, interpretive trails, visitor center, and gift shop. A modern museum on the grounds features the multimedia exhibit: *Sacred Encounters: Father DeSmet and the Indians of the Rocky Mountain West.*

The Old Mission was a spiritual center and wayside rest stop along the Mullan Road, where an eclectic mix of Indians, priests, soldiers, prospectors, and entrepreneurs found hospitality and shared stories on any given night. It was a staging area for pack trains heading to the Eagle City gold camp, and the head of navigation for steamboats from Lake Coeur d'Alene. The Wyatt Earp family was among the throngs who disembarked here and spent a cold winter's night in a tent before proceeding on horseback to Eagle City, where Earp opened a saloon called the White Elephant.

The park is an easy ride 3.5 miles west of Cataldo Trailhead. Turn left from the trailhead, cross the bridge over the Coeur d'Alene River, and travel west on Canyon Rd. for 2.2 miles. Go left on Dredge Rd. and proceed another mile to the I-90 overpass, then follow the sign. Summer hours are: 9 a.m. to 5 p.m., April through October. $5 to enter park/$5 to enter the museum. Call 208.682.3814 for more information. Find them on Facebook.

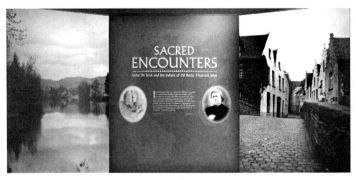

Trail Miles: 43.6 — Pine Meadows Scenic Wayside

WHERE AM I?
The north bank of the Coeur d'Alene River in Shoshone County.

REST AREA AMENITIES:
Picnic Table.
Next Stop: .7 mile

Trail Miles: 44.3 — Gap Rock Scenic Wayside

WHERE AM I?
The north bank of the Coeur d'Alene River in Shoshone County.

REST AREA AMENITIES:
Picnic Table, Interpretive Sign.
Next Stop: 1.2 miles

Backwater Bay Scenic Wayside
Trail Miles: 45.5

On the trial between Cataldo and Pine Meadows

WHERE AM I?
The north bank of the Coeur d'Alene River in Shoshone County.

REST AREA AMENITIES:
Picnic Table, Interpretive Sign.
Next Stop: 1.6 miles

Trail Miles: 47.1 — Enaville Trailhead

DRIVING DIRECTIONS: From I-90 take Kingston Exit #43 and head north 1.2 miles up the Coeur d'Alene River Rd. The trailhead is on the left.

TRAILHEAD AMENITIES: Restroom/Accessible, Picnic Table, Interpretive Sign, 10 Parking Spaces/1 ADA. (Food nearby).
Next Stop: 1.6 miles.

ELEVATION: 2,224 FT. — Kingston, Idaho (Enaville)

The north and south forks of the Coeur d'Alene River converge by the unincorporated town of Kingston, in Shoshone County. The trailhead overlooks a habitat rich with migratory songbirds and the interpretive sign helps you identify them by their singing styles.

Many cyclists have wined and dined at the **Enaville Resort,** a.k.a. The Snakepit. When former owners and avid trail supporters, Joe and Rose Mary Peak, passed away in 2012, the place closed, then changed hands. It's for sale again, but open and serving food as of this writing. Call 208.682.3453 for updates.

Kingston, Idaho/Enaville

Point of Interest: The Schitsu'umsch tribal chief and prophet, Circling Raven, was buried near Kingston in 1760. He had foreseen the coming of the Black Robes and had told his people about the Savior of the World. After returning from a bison hunt in the Great Plains in 1740, his group set up a winter camp in the vicinity of what is now Kingston — or *The King's Town*. A Coeur d'Alene tradition says they celebrated their first Christmas here that year, 100 years before the first Jesuits arrived.

Point of Interest: The discovery of gold up the North Fork in the early 1880s caused a stampede of hopeful gold miners to the Coeur d'Alene Mountains. When the gold diggings played out, many men turned to logging to earn a living. That's when annual log drives became a common sight on the river. The workers upriver needed supplies, so several profitable packstrings flourished around Enaville in the early days. The town boomed when construction started on the Idaho Northern Railroad up the North Fork. At one time, two thousand men lived in railroad labor camps that dotted the river.

Upper Enaville was a half mile north of the Snakepit, at McFee Gulch. By 1910 buildings included the Finn Worker's Lodge, six saloons where thirty prostitutes plied their trade, a grocery store, and post office. The vintage grocery store that once stood on this side of the river played a role in the movie *Dante's Peak*. It was later floated across the river and added to Albert's place. Most of Enaville was swept away by the flood of 1933.

For RV and tent camping, and to catch the **river float** bus at **Alberts**, ride .5 mile north on the Coeur d'Alene River Rd. then turn right and loop over the wooden plank bridge.

From Enaville Trailhead, it's a flat and scenic 6-mile ride along the North Fork of the Coeur d'Alene River to the **Country Lane Resort.** Cross the bridge .5 mile north of the trail and ride the Old River Road to the resort. To drive there from I-90, take Exit #43 and follow the Coeur d'Alene River Rd. north 5.5 miles to Bumblebee turnoff. Turn right after the bridge to the Old River Rd. and go 1.9 miles. Check in at the restaurant.

"Shoe Tree" at Alberts with old store from Dante's Peak in the background.

Country Lane Resort & Event Center

Country Lane Resort is a rustic and laid back destination on the North Fork of the Coeur d'Alene River. It is an ideal spot for travelers to get off the beaten path to **dine**, relax, **hike**, **swim**, **fish**, or **float** the river. The roomy **B&B**, **vacation suite,** and **campground** can easily accommodate large groups. The B&B features king beds, indoor **hot tub**, and **breakfast anytime** in the restaurant. When making reservations, lodging guests may request a **courtesy pickup** from the Enaville Trailhead.

The **restaurant** and **lounge** attract many repeat visitors who return from miles around to enjoy a meal from Peggy's kitchen, where the specialties include certified Angus beef, and fresh made soups, garden salads, and side dishes. Dine on the spacious covered deck, or gather around the fire to tell stories and sing songs.

Some RV sites have full hookups. Bathrooms and hot showers on site. Spots on the river have 50/30/20 amp power and water, and an outdoor bar and stage for live music events. There is also a 35-acre outdoor **event center for reunions and retreats**. For details and reservations, call Peggy Morris **1.877.670.5927.**

B&B (sleeps 20 plus)
King Beds, Kitchens
Fireplace, Satellite
DVD/VCR, Views
Honeymoon Suite
Vacation Suite
RV Sites with P/W
Full Hookups

www.countrylaneresort.com   stay@countrylaneresort.com

Pine Creek Trailhead   Trail Miles: 48.7

DRIVING DIRECTIONS: Take I-90 to the Pinehurst/Smelterville Exit #45. The trailhead is north on the Coeur d'Alene River.

TRAILHEAD AMENITIES: Picnic Table, Interpretive Sign, 15 Parking Spaces/ 1 ADA. (Food, Camping, Shopping, Showers, Laundry, Post Office nearby). **Next Stop: 2.4 miles**

Pinehurst, Idaho   ELEVATION: 2,224 FT.

The City of Pinehurst, pop. 1,619, is on the south side of the Coeur d'Alene River in Shoshone County. Take the paved bike path south along Little Pine Creek, .4 mile to **Brewed Awakening** espresso stand at Heritage Park and **By The Way Campground** across N. Division St.

By the Way Campground is nestled against the hillside right off the trail. Cabin and camping options include a bunk-house style **camping cabin** with power, drinking water, microwave, coffee pot, and mini-fridge, (you provide the bedding), and another larger cabin with kitchenette, a half-bath, two full-sized beds, couches, and two TVs. The shower house and restroom are steps away. 13 **RV spaces** have water and electric. (No sewer hookups, but there is a dump station on site); seven tent sites, several with picnic tables and fire pits. Non-guests can **shower** for a small fee. Thirsty trail riders are welcome to stop by and fill water bottles here.

Rv & Tent Sites
Two Cabins
Shower House

Shoshone County Park is one block past the campground. It's a peaceful place to picnic in the grass. Find **public restrooms** there. Call 208.753.5475 to check park hours. The **Laundromat** is across the street. **The Tall Pine** eatery is .5 mile south of the campground. Check them out for burgers, sandwiches, shakes and more. For **Barney's Harvest Foods** turn into the parking lot just

Pinehurst, Idaho

past the Tall Pine. They are a full service grocer and carry some locally grown produce in season. For the **post office**, turn right on Main.

Back on the trail, Before Smelterville, you will come to a **Walmart.** A ramp leads from the trail into the parking lot and a bike rack near the front entrance. Restrooms are ADA accessible. Three-tenths of a mile further east is the Silver Valley Office Coeur d'Alene Ranger Station for the Idaho National Forest. Check the outdoor rack of **visitor information** on everything from medicinal wildflowers to gold panning in the forest. Also see: fs.usda.gov/activity/ipnf/recreation.

Trail Miles: 51.1 ## Smelterville Trailhead

DRIVING DIRECTIONS: Take I-90 to exit #48 and turn south. Trailhead parking is on your left before the stop sign at Main St.

TRAILHEAD AMENITIES: Portable Toilet, Bench, 17 Parking Spaces/none marked ADA. No overnight parking. Food, Water. (Post Office nearby). **Next Stop: 2 miles**

Smelterville, Idaho
ELEVATION: 2,224 FT.

The City of Smelterville, pop. 621, is on the south side of I-90 in Shoshone County. If you began in Plummer, you have pedaled slightly more than fifty miles. Reward yourself at **The Espresso Barn.** It's right on the trail across from the mine car display at the city's entrance. The folks at the Espresso Barn have been serving the Silver Valley for more than a decade and have many satisfied customers. The delicious peanut butter cup granita is a popular favorite. They also serve iced lattés, espresso shakes, Chai tea, Italian sodas, juice, muffins, bagels, biscotti, and cookies. They open early daily. If you are riding with a large group you may call in your order and tell them your estimated time of arrival.

Back on the trail there is a Dept. of Parks and Rec. shop with a water spigot .46 miles east of Smelterville where bottles can be refilled.

Silver Mountain Trailhead   Trail Miles: 53.1

DRIVING DIRECTIONS: Take I-90 Exit #49 to Bunker Ave./Silver Mountain. Turn south over the Coeur d'Alene River and go .4 mile to the large parking lot on your right, across from Gondola Village. There is no sign that marks this as a trailhead.

North America's Longest Gondola at Silver Mountain, Kellogg, Idaho

TRAILHEAD AMENITIES: Benches, Picnic Tables, BBQ Stands, Interpretive Signs. (Restroom, Water, Food, Lodging, Swimming, Shopping, Museum, Rentals nearby). The Gondola Village parking lot is indistinguishable from trailhead parking. There are no ADA designated parking spaces. RVs should park on the far end of the lot, away from the resort and gondola area. **Next Stop: .7 mile**

Kellogg, Idaho   ELEVATION: 2,308 FT.

The City of Kellogg, pop. 2,117, lies along the Coeur d'Alene River in Shoshone County, Kellogg. The **indoor water park, skate park, gold mine tour**, and one of the Northwest's top **lift-served mountain bike parks** make it a natural stop for families exploring the trail with kids.

The nearest services are across the street from the trailhead in Gondola Village. Find public **restrooms** next to the gondola boarding station just past **Noah's restaurant**. Gondola Village has lodging a water park, several eateries, and a sporting good store. There is an **ATM** in the lodge lobby.

Point of Interest: You can't be in Kellogg long without hearing about how the town owes its existence to a jackass—or donkey, for those who prefer the more delicate term. (The perfectly correct word for the animal is simply *ass*—derived from the official *Equus Asinus*). An ass that carried Noah Kellogg's grubstake on a prospecting trip in 1884, is said to have stumbled upon an outcropping of galena near Milo Creek. Long story short, The Bunker Hill Company sprang into existence and silver and lead ore worth millions has been extracted from rich underground veins.

The township of Kellogg was organized in 1892 and for many years "Uncle Bunker" was a generous benefactor to the welfare of its citizens by providing both good-paying jobs and perks, like a YMCA, and major contributions for the ski hill (formerly the Jackass Bowl) built in 1968.

Kellogg, Idaho

There are several lodging choices close to the Silver Mountain Trailhead. **Guesthouse Inn and Suites** on the east edge has an **indoor pool**, hot tub, secure bicycle storage, and continental breakfast.

Take the path south from the trailhead to **Silver Ridge**, where condo suites beckon to travelers who like a bit of luxury with their cycling. See pictures and make reservations at kelloggvacationhomes.com.

Accommodations at the **Morning Star Lodge** in Gondola Village include **studios, suites**, and **rooftop hot tubs.** You can see virtual tours at silvermt.com under the lodging/floor plans link. Secure storage for cycle equipment is included with your room. The lodge is a 2014 Trip Advisor Certificate of Excellence Winner. Lodging guests have access to Silver Rapids, Idaho's largest **indoor waterpark**, which offers amenities for all ages, from the tiny tots Pollywog Pond, to the Trestles bar, where patrons can soak in a hot tub overlooking The waterpark and sip drinks while watching people surf and body board on the FlowRider® wave. Dining choices at **Noah's Canteen** include steaks, fish, pasta dishes, fresh seasonal vegetables, wraps, pizzas, sandwiches, and decadent desserts. See **online menu** at silvermt.com, under the *Amenities* link. The outdoor fireplaces are a nice touch, as are the anti-prohibition photos in the full service lounge.

Silver Mountain Sports in Gondola Village is a sales rental and repair shop with pavement **bikes**, trailers, and a new fleet of mountain bikes for use in the Silver Mountain Bike Park. Comfortable *Specialized* cycle rentals for the Trail of the Coeur d'Alenes come with a helmet. The **apparel and accessory** selection includes Dakine, Fox, Giro, Smith, Oakley, and The North Face.

Here is a convenient Connecting Trip that will make you a hero with the kids. Take a 20-minute ride on North America's **longest gondola** for a day of mountain top fun. Park your road bikes at Gondola Village, switch out for some **mountain bike** gear at Silver Mountain Sports, and enjoy a thrilling day at **Silver Mountain Bike Park**, named by riders among the best in the Northwest. Choose from more than 30 downhill trails, where seasoned riders appreciate the variety of super flowy single track, rough, technical fall-line trails and machine built, hand-tuned jump lines. Beginners can ease into it with a mix of single and double track trails in the "Chair 3 Zone" with access to a shorter portion of the mountain that has plenty of options for all ability levels.

Those who enjoy recreating at a mellower pace can enjoy a **gondola ride** to beautiful interpretive **nature trails**, visit the Mountain House Grill, play some disc golf, and pick **wild berries** in late summer. (Watch for bears because they like them too). Do the **Ride and Dine** on Fridays, from late June to August, for live music and a savory barbecue dinner with all the fixings in a mountain top setting. The summer-time gondola schedule starts in mid-June and runs through the first weekend in October. See details on the August **Brewfest** and other mountain activities at silvermt.com/Outdoor Adventures. Top off your Silver Mountain visit with a night at Morning Star Lodge and a day of play at Silver Rapids water park.

SILVER
Mountain Resort
SILVERMT.COM
(866) 345-2675

PHOTO COURTESY OF SILVER MT

- 52 -

Kellogg, Idaho

The bike trail runs east behind the Guesthouse Inn and cuts through the center of town between Historic Uptown Kellogg and the newer section along I-90. Exploring this section of the trail continues on the next page. Meanwhile, if you have a craving for **McDonalds** or **Subway**, head north on Bunker Ave. over I-90 to Cameron Ave. This is also the street to find authentic **Mexican dining**, and other restaurants, groceries, a drug store/variety store, and more lodgings.

Turn right on Cameron to find **Silver Horn Motor Inn**, a locally-owned motel and adjoining restaurant. There may be barking dogs that greet you when arriving at the guest desk. The Silverhorn offers a **16-foot swim spa** and free **Wifi, DVD library**, and **laundry** facility. All rooms have air-conditioning, microwave, and mini-fridge. Bicycles are allowed in rooms. Coffee is in the lobby 24 hrs. a day. Call 1.800.437.6437 for reservations. The adjacent **Silver Spoon Restaurant** serves breakfast, lunch and dinner. It's known for its generous portions, huge cinnamon roles, homemade pies, and pancakes made with locally picked huckleberries. Summer hours are 6 a.m. to 8 p.m. daily. Room service is available during restaurant hours.

Ride east to Hill St. for the Trail Motel, IGA grocery store, and variety/drug store at that intersection. The motel is under new management. Rooms still start at $40 plus tax.

Casa de Oro at 120 W. Cameron has delicious **Mexican** lunch and dinner specialties. The friendly service, relaxing atmosphere, and the best of old Mexico's recipes, make this a popular spot among locals and visitors alike. If you've worked up an appetite on the trail, you will appreciate their huge selection of Mexican-style beef, pork, chicken, seafood, egg, and vegetarian dishes. For dessert, it's hard

Kellogg, Idaho

to choose between a creamy flan, apple burrito with caramel sauce and whipped cream, or deep fried ice cream.

Going south on Hill St. leads back to the trail. After the I-90 underpass, there will be a **Yoke's** grocery store on the right. On the next block, look for **Hill Street Depot** on River St. across from the city park. They specialize in meat dishes paired with **microbrews** from North Idaho Mountain Brewery in Wallace. Hill Street Depot has outdoor seating and **Wifi**. Check out the unique fence made with bombs at the veteran's memorial park between the Depot and the trail.

Kellogg's **Historic Uptown** is straight up Hill Street, with shops, restaurants, and services, including the **post office, museum,** and **library**. This is where you will find **Dirty Ernie's bar, The Pizza Palace, Moose Creek Grill, Wahing Chinese Restaurant, Kellogg Vacation Homes** rentals, and the **skate park**. You could pedal past the ball field straight up Hill St. to McKinley, but it's much easier to take the short path from Silver Mountain Trailhead. It's also the easiest way to reach the **Staff House Museum** and The Ridge condos.

Path from the Trail of the Coeur d'Alenes to Shoshone County Mining & Smelting Museum, aka The Staff House Museum

Ride west on the trail from Hill St. through the park. You will pass the city pool and **Bunker Place**, a roomy **Kellogg Vacation Home** that sits right on the trail across from the community garden.

Back at Silver Mountain Trailhead, take the path that leads south to the **Shoshone County Mining & Smelting Museum** also known as the Staff House. A stop here will deepen your appreciation of the Silver Valley's rough and tumble mining history, its colorful characters, and the martial law that was instituted when mining disputes erupted in the 1890s. The building was originally constructed in 1906 as a residence for Bunker Hill Mine Manager, Stanley Easton and his wife. The gift shop selection includes history books by local authors and silver jewelry. They are open May through Sept. 10 a.m. to 6 p.m. closed Tues. 208.556.1592.

Ride east on McKinley past Hill St. and the ball park for shops and services in Uptown Kellogg. **Dirty Ernie's** is a friendly full-service

Kellogg, Idaho

lounge with a nice view of Kellogg from inside or on the deck. There is a birds eye view of Teeter's ball field down below, so the town folks gather here to drink while they watch the kids play. It's a great place to sample the locally brewed Loft Honey Belgian pale ale from the North Idaho Mountain Brewery in Wallace. The XM Satellite tunes are always on and live music acts entertain about once a month. Despite the name, the place is very clean, but the posters on the restroom walls are not for the easily flustered.

Wah Hing one block east, is the only Chinese restaurant on the trail. Some say this family-owned establishment is the best place to get Chinese in North Idaho.

Point of Interest: If you have heard the Silver Valley is one of the richest silver mining districts in the world, you may be asking yourself where all the silver is, and why this neighborhood has many empty stores. The rich silver deposits are embedded in a nine mile-wide swath between Pinehurst and the Montana state line. The ground beneath you is laced with hundreds of miles of interconnecting tunnels that reach 10,000 feet deep in some places—and there are hundreds of people working down there as we speak. More than 1.2 billion troy ounces of silver have been blasted and hauled out of these mountains since old Kellogg's donkey first stumbled on the galena outcropping.

Much of the silver is in demand for products like cell phones and solar panels. A little trickles back to the valley in the form of commemorative rounds produced at Sunshine Minting in Coeur d'Alene. You can get these collectors' medallions at gift shops along the trail.

So why the empty storefronts amidst all this wealth? For one thing, where there were once dozens of mines in the area, now there are only four. Many of today's miners commute from the Coeur d'Alene area and do their shopping closer to home. This, combined with

Kellogg, Idaho

The Clock Tower

strict environmental rules demanded by the EPA translate to higher costs of doing business that can be a strain on the Valley's businesses.

Look for the **The Pizza Palace** under the clock tower on the corner of Main and McKinley for **pizzas, calzones, pasta dishes, pita pockets, salads espresso,** and **fresh baked pastries.** The addition of beer and wine is anticipated at time of writing.

Queen Eileen will make you feel welcome as she creates pizzas named for precious stones, like garnet (BBQ Chicken with mozzarella, onions, bacon, and cheddar), and sapphire (pepperoni with onion, mushrooms, olives, sausage, mozzarella, and pizza sauce). Order a custom pizza or dragon eggs (calzones) from any of the meats, veggies, and specialty toppings. Create your own salad too. Just circle the ingredients you want and they will build it. If you don't feel like going out after a long day on the trail, give them a call. **Delivery** is offered along the Trail of the Coeur d'Alenes between the Kingston Post Office and Harvest Foods in Wallace. They are open seven days a week and also have **free Wifi.** Like them on Facebook to keep track of specials and to see photos of the menu.

Access the connecting shops at **Main Street Market** from inside The Pizza Palace, where two floors of intriguing vintage, collectible, and secondhand items are displayed for sale. Don't miss the **waterfall** and **mine tunnel replica** in **Pappa's Barn** basement.

Point of Interest: The lobby of the **Kellogg Post Office,** next block south on Division and Portland, features a historic mural of Noah Kellogg and his donkey. This work by Fletcher Martin is one of six WPA murals in Idaho. His original submission depicted a wounded miner being carried on a stretcher. The townspeople protested, saying it would be too depressing to have to look at every time they had business in the post office. So, this design, with a more lighthearted theme was chosen instead.

The Pizza Palace

Delivery from Kingston to Wallace

7 Days a Week

208-783-1323

Kellogg, Idaho

Moose Creek Grill is a five-star restaurant with a 2014 Certificate of Excellence from Trip Advisor.

Kellogg's finest dinner house is at the end of McKinley on Division. The **Moose Creek Grill** has a great selection of steak, fresh seafood, pasta dishes with **handmade pastas**, and **vegetarian** options cooked to perfection. Feast on a mouth-watering charbroiled Angus prime rib-eye **steak** with garden **wild rice** or Parmesan-garlic mashed potatoes.

Owners, Joel and Betsy, take great pride in the sauces, and desserts **prepared from scratch**. They offer an extensive wine list and a variety of beers in the bottle and on tap from **Wallace Brewing Co.** Enjoy your meal on the veranda, or surrounded by the family-friendly country ambiance inside. See the **menu online** at moosecreekgrill.com. Reservations are recommended but not required.

Point of Interest: Once a raucous mining town, Wardner (pop. 185) is now a calm residential area on the southwest end of Division St. The settlement sprang up around the prolific Bunker Hill mine. Namesake, Jim Wardner, had arrived in Eagle City during the gold rush of '83, with 200 pounds of butter that he pulled over the pass from Thompson Falls, Montana, through 20 feet of snow. He sold the butter to gold-crazed miners and used the proceeds to set up a successful pack train for people rushing to the gold fields. Always the entreprenurial opportunist, Wardner leveraged himself into the Bunker Hill venture by sneakily claiming water rights to Kellogg's mining claim. He found investors to develop the mine and by 1931, Bunker Hill had 1300 employees.

Kellogg has a small **skate park** on Main and Division. You can find a **public restroom** there as well. Several Kellogg Vacation Homes are in this residential neighborhood between the uptown business area and Wardner.

Fine Family Dining

MOOSE CREEK GRILL

Open at 4:00 Wednesday ~ Sunday
208.783.2625 ~ moosecreekgrill.com
Division & Portland in Kellogg, Idaho

Home Sweet Home Base for a Rail-Trail Vacation

The Summit is one of the four cabins at Backwoods Alley in Kellogg

Kellogg Vacation Homes specializes in well-appointed vacation rentals that are clean and cozy with all the conveniences of home. In many cases you can rent an entire house for the cost of a motel room, a particularly smart solution for groups. Most are remodeled older homes. Here are some examples of KVH rentals within a mile of the trail. A cluster of four homes is tucked against the mountainside a few blocks from historic uptown Kellogg at **Backwoods Alley**. They are near good restaurants and interesting shops, and close to the skate park, which will keep the kids entertained. All homes include full kitchens, gas fireplace, washer/dryer, stereo, VCR, wireless Internet, and gas barbecue. Most have a dishwasher, and each has its own **hot tub**. The Backwoods also has a pool table. There is plenty of covered cycle parking. Starting at $60 per night.

Mooster Lodge provides the best of both worlds. It's like a home in the country with plenty of space to enjoy the outdoors, yet only two blocks to shops and restaurants. This 3 bedroom, 2 bath home has all the modern conveniences. It also features a wood fireplace, cycle storage, covered deck and hot tub with a view.

Mooster Lodge

Bunker Place is in the heart of the action, right on the Trail of the Coeur d'Alenes and a block from Silver Mountain's Gondola Village. This modern 3-bedroom, 3-bath tri-level sleeps eight. It has two gas fireplaces, a full kitchen, hot tub, deck, and jetted tub. There is plenty of secure indoor storage space for your cycles and gear.

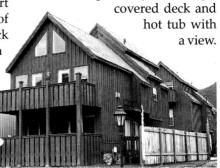

Bunker Place is steps from the trail

The Mill House

Bring the family to the charming **Mill House** with a white picket fence that says welcome to small town America. It is also in historic uptown Kellogg, just a half mile from the trail and ski hill. Like all the Kellogg Vacation Homes, the kitchen is stocked with everything you need except for groceries. Washer/dryer, gas fireplace, barbecue, VCR, Wifi, and private covered hot tub.

The **Lazy Bear** home sleeps nine and has all the amenities you need , including, 2.5 baths, washer/dryer, game room with bar and pool table, hot tub, and gas barbecue. This home is an easy, flat ride from the trail, near grocery stores and restaurants on Kellogg's north side.

Lazy Bear

Kellogg Vacation homes has numerous other rental homes in the Silver Valley, and owner Francine is also a real estate agent. So if you're looking to stay for a night or forever, give her a call at 800.435.2588 or visit the office in the **Kellogg-Warner Depot** right on the trail. See inside the homes at kelloggvacation homes.com.

Kellogg Vacation Homes   800-435-2588
kelloggvacationhomes.com   10 E Station Ave, Kellogg, ID 83837

To return to the trail from Historic Uptown Kellogg, ride downhill (north) on Division to the trail crossing. The trailhead is about a half block west of the Kellogg-Wardner train depot. Stairs from the parking area lead to the historic uptown district.

Trail Miles: 53.8   Kellogg Depot Trailhead

DRIVING DIRECTIONS: Take I-90 to Exit #51, Division St./Wardner. Go south on Division, cross the trail, and turn right across from the Depot after the bicycle sign. Trail parking is at the far end of the parking area.

TRAILHEAD AMENITIES: Trail Info Interpretive Sign, Bench. Parking/none marked ADA. (Restroom, Water, Food, Lodging, Shopping, Rentals, Laundry, Post Office, Visitor Info. nearby).
Next Stop: 1.4 miles

Kellogg, Idaho

EXCELSIOR CYCLE is right on the Trail of the Coeur d'Alenes, between the trailhead and Kellogg-Warner Depot. Owners Mike and Debbie Domy have served the region's cycling community for more than two decades. They **sell, rent**, and expertly **service** a variety of **cycles**. Dedicated repeat customers come from as far as Spokane, Seattle, Portland, Canada, and beyond, to benefit from Mike's fair prices, technical knowledge, and skill. They are open year round and carry a wide selection of **gear**. The folks here are a great source of **information** about the local cycling scene.

Point of Interest: Excelsior Cycle is in a former train depot that was built sometime between 1909 and 1914. An earlier depot stood here when the mining district came under martial law in 1892. Four companies of Fourth Infrantry soldiers deployed from Fort Sherman detrained here and built a makeshit stockade, also known as "the bullpen," along the railroad tracks. Some 1,000 protesting labor union miners were rounded up and imprisoned there in harsh conditions.

What is there to do when visiting Kellogg?

Recreation
Disc Golf
Skate Park
Golf Courses
Walking Trails
Mountain Bike Park
Trail of the Coeur d'Alenes
Biggest Indoor Water Park
North America's Longest Gondola

Dining
American, Mexican, Greek
Chinese, Pizza & Pasta

*Ride & Dine
on Silver Mountain
Fridays in Summer*

Tours & Museums
Crystal Gold Mine
Fire Lookout Self Tour
Staff House Mining Museum

Shopping *Find Treasures Uptown & Downtown
in Kellogg's Gift, Collectible,
and Specialty Shops*

KELLOGG · WARDNER

See us for all your Kellogg area vacation needs!

HISTORIC SILVER VALLEY CHAMBER OF COMMERCE
In the Kellogg-Wardner Depot **208-784-0821**

kelloggidaho.org ✳ director@silvervalleychamber.com
Exit 51 on I-90 or mile marker 53.8 on the Trail of the Coeur d'Aenes

HISTORIC SILVER VALLEY CHAMBER OF COMMERCE

Elizabeth Park Trailhead   Trail Miles: 55.2

DRIVING DIRECTIONS: From I-90 take Division St./Warder Exit #51, north to Cameron. Turn east, drive 1.3 miles parallel to the freeway. (It turns into Silver Valley Rd.). See Crystal Gold Mine at MP 52. Turn right across from the RV park and go under I-90 overpass at Elizabeth Park Rd. Trailhead is on the left.

TRAILHEAD AMENITIES: Picnic Table, Interpretive Sign, 20 Parking Spaces/None Marked ADA. (Camping, Mine Tour, Gift Shop, nearby) **Next Stop: 2.2 miles**

Take an underground tour of the **Crystal Gold Mine**, just a short pedal north of the trailhead. See shiny deposits of gold and silver in the mine walls. Get an hour of free gold panning (seasonal) with mine tour. Open 7-days a week, Feb. 14 to Dec. 31. Summer hours are 9 a.m. to 6 p.m. Adults $12/Kids $8.50. RV camping on site. 208.783.4653.

Shont Trailhead   Trail Miles: 57.4

Memorial to fallen miners of the Sunshine Mine disaster

DRIVING DIRECTIONS: From I-90 take Big Creek Exit #54. The trailhead is south of the Interstate along the river.

TRAILHEAD AMENITIES: Picnic Table, Interpretive Sign. 20 Parking Spaces/1 ADA. Miner Memorial attraction. **Next Stop: 3 miles**

Big Creek

Ride north under the freeway to the **Sunshine Mine Monument**. The hum of I-90 traffic drowns into the background at this solemn spot that honors ninety-one miners who lost their lives in a catastrophic accident at the Sunshine Mine in 1972.

As you shop at local grocery stores or relax in the restaurants, consider that many of the people you brush shoulders with, or their families and friends, have spent a hard life working underground. Most Silver Valley families lost friends and loved ones at the tragic Sunshine Mine accident.

Point of Interest: Booming silver prices prompted the incorporation of Sunshine Mining Co. in 1918. The company employed 450 local workers, and produced more than 400,000 ounces of silver each month. More than 360,000,000 ounces were produced in all.

Osburn, Idaho

Osburn's **Gene Day Park** is before the next trailhead. It has tennis and basketball courts, volleyball net, playground, **water** fountains, **picnic areas**, BBQ pits, and **public restrooms** with one ADA accessible. The park is open daily May 1 through Sept. 30, from 7 a.m. to 8 p.m.

Numerous streets cross the trail in Osburn, each one with a stop sign. If you're camping at **Blue Anchor RV Park**, turn left onto Yellowstone at the fifth stop sign, 1.2 miles after Gene Day Park. Look for the bridge on your right and a small city park. The Blue Anchor is across the street. Blue Anchor has **RV** and tent **camping** with nice grassy spots in the shade, **showers**, **laundry**, **visitor information**, and **Wifi**. 208.752.3443.

Trail Miles: 60.4   Osburn Trailhead

DRIVING DIRECTIONS: Take I-90 to Exit #57 and follow I-90 BL south to Mullan Ave. Turn left on Mullan and right on Sixth St. to the trailhead.

TRAILHEAD AMENITIES: Picnic Table, Interpretive Sign, 9 Parking Spaces/1 ADA. (Bottled Water, Food, Camping, Shopping, Post Office nearby). **Next Stop: 4.2 miles**

Osburn, Idaho   Elevation 2,520 FT.

The City of Osburn, pop. 1,545, is on the south side of I-90 in Shoshone County. Ride north one block on Sixth St. from the trailhead to access stores, banks, and other services on Mullan Ave. Turn right on Mullan and go one block to **Mom's Vintage Eatery,** which serves breakfast, lunch, and dinner daily from 8 a.m. to 8 p.m.

Stein's Market grocery store with deli is across the street. You can also get postage stamps here and stock up on **bottled water**. **Osburn Drug** next door carries clothing, fishing licenses, and sundries. Go the other way for **espresso** at **Capparelli's** on third. The **Laundromat** and **post office** are on the way. If you keep going west a few more blocks, you'll come to the Blue Anchor campground.

Ride 3.2 miles past the Osburn Trailhead to a stop sign where the trail crosses Silver Valley Rd. A mile farther look for a small sign that says **"Welcome to Wallace."**

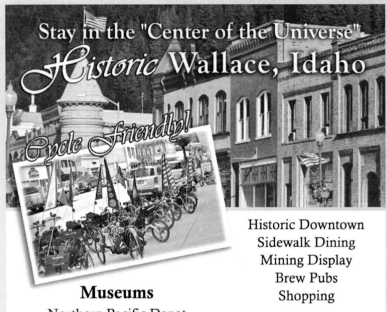

Mining Heritage Exhibit at the Wallace Visitor Center

Wallace, Idaho

Turn south and cycle under I-90 to access the Historic Wallace Chamber of Commerce **Visitor Center**. See the free outdoor **Mining Heritage Exhibit**. The volunteer-run visitor center is open daily during summer. **Bottled water** is sold inside. Get **regional visitor information** and view **menus** for all the restaurants in town. The **public restrooms** are open year round, 24-hours a day. For information, call 208.751.7151 during business hours.

The **Wallace Inn and Trailside Café** are one block east of the visitor center on Front St. along the river. The Wallace Inn received certificates of excellence from AAA and TripAdvisor in 2014. Motel manager Rick Shaffer is the "Prime Minister" of both Historic Wallace and the Coeur d'Alene Trails. His primary objective is to assure that cyclists visiting Historic Wallace have the most memorable bike adventure possible. So, feel free to call him at 208.752.1252 with all your questions.

Wallace, Idaho

Wallace Inn guests arriving by airplane may inquire about the **shuttle service** from Spokane International Airport when making reservations. Guests cycling from another trailhead can arrange to be shuttled back to their vehicle. If you want more time for rest and recreation in the **indoor pool, hot tub, steamroom, dry sauna,** or **weight/exercise room** they will have someone drive your car to Wallace. **Shuttles to the Route of the Hiawatha** may also be reserved in the brand new 2014 extended van with trailer. Guests who want to rent equip-

Indoor pool, jacuzzi and sauna at Wallace Inn

ment from **Excelsior Cycle** can ask for a ride to Kellogg as well. There is convenient and **secure indoor storage** for your cycle equipment

The Inn's spacious rooms have king and queen beds, 32-inch flat screen TVs, mini-fridges, in-room coffee, hair dryers, irons, and free **Wifi**. The Wallace Inn is **pet-friendly**. A gift section in the lobby stocks local history books, post cards, huckleberry chocolates and jams, silver and garnet jewelry, and **commemorative rail trail silver rounds**. Enjoy the view through the adjoining four-season windows at the bright **Trailside Café** where waffles, pancakes, French toast, eggs, omelettes, meats, and potatoes are on the breakfast menu, 7 a.m. to 11 a.m daily, and there is full service until 8 p.m.

Inquire about **recreational packages** with the Route of the Hiawatha, Silver Streak Zipline Tours, White Water Rafting and Fly Fishing on the St. Joe, Clark Fork, and Coeur d'Alene Rivers. See thewallace inn.com for details, or call 208.691.9169.

Point of Interest: Wallace was a cedar swamp surrounded by a dense forest when Colonel W.R. Wallace arrived in 1884 to locate the town, initially called Placer Center. Wallace and his companions dragged their belongings over the snow on toboggans, traveling at night in an attempt to ditch men who thought they were headed for secret gold deposits. Wallace correctly predicted this place would become the "center of one of the richest mining sections of this continent." The town prospered but the Colonel (who was not a real colonel) was less fortunate. The scrip he had used to acquire the land turned out to be worthless. One day in March of 1889, when the townspeople discovered this fact, they surprised Wallace by jumping all his claims. "After I have proven the prophecy of five years ago...they would rob me of what little I have left of the hardships and privations of pioneering," he lamented.

For lodging at the **Hercules Inn,** leave the trail at the Visitor Center as well, and go to the block past the Wallace Inn. The Victorian Inn has spacious 500-sq. ft. suites with homey décor. They have firm king & queen beds, Direct TV on flat screens in the bedroom and living room, **free WiFi**, and **laundry**. Cook on the **barbecue** or in the kitchen, which is fully stocked with everything but the groceries. Relax on one of the decks or in the **hot tub** outside. There is covered parking for cycles. Daily and weekly rates. Call 208.556.0575 for reservations.

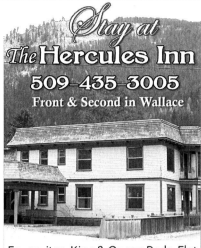

To get to the Historic Wallace 6th Street Trailhead return to the trail by the visitor center and ride under Wallace's famous freeway a half mile to the trailhead. See the **City Limits Pub & Grill** and **Wallace RV Park** adjacent to the trailhead parking area.

Historic Wallace 6th St. Trailhead   Trail Miles: 64.6

DRIVING DIRECTIONS: Take I-90 to Exit #62, Wallace/Burke and take Bank St. to 6th St. Turn right and go past the Northern Pacific Depot Railroad Museum. Trailhead is on the right, over the bridge.

TRAILHEAD AMENITIES: Interpretive Sign, 6 Parking Spaces/2 Accessible. (Restroom, Water, Museum, at NP Depot Museum. Food, Lodging, Camping, Swimming, Shopping, Museums, Tours, Showers, Laundry, Post Office nearby).
Next Stop: 1.3 miles

Northern Pacific Depot Museum across the river from the trailhead is a visitor center with public restroom and drinking water

Wallace, Idaho ELEVATION: 2,744 FT.

Wallace, Idaho, pop. 784, is the Shoshone County seat. The entire downtown is listed on the National Historic Register and the community has a great mix of historical architecture. It's easy to spend several days browsing, eating, and having fun in and around Wallace.

You can see **City Limits Pub & Grill** and **microbrewery** to the north of the trailhead. The non-smoking restaurant and bar includes a beautifully handcrafted bar made from a slab of burled white pine. The menu ranges from Brewers Scotch eggs to broasted chicken, and includes **vegetarian** and **gluten free** choices. See the menu at citylimitspub andgrill.com. Get a sampler of eight **North Idaho Mountain Brew** craft beers for $12. You can also get a 64-oz. refillable growler to go. The adjacent **Wallace RV Park** has 43 full hookups, **tent sites,** and three non-smoking **camping cabins** that accommodate from three to five guests. Bring your own sleeping pads and bedding. The bathroom/shower facility is **ADA accessible.** You can **shower** for a fee even if you are not camping. This is a **pet-friendly** establishment.

Northern Pacific Depot is a block south of the trailhead on Sixth St. You will find displays about the area's **railroad history, visitor information,** a **drinking water fountain,** and **public restrooms.** The featured exhibit in 2015 is *"Wallace Promotions,"* a collection of matchbooks, tokens, pens, pins, and other memorabilia from the historical business district. Shop for **souvenirs, T-shirts, locally-made items,** and **history books.** The museum is open daily May through October and hosts several events throughout the year. It is also available for private events, such as weddings. Depot Days is May 9th in 2015, and Under the Freeway Flea Market is Sept. 5 to 7. See npdepot.org for *In the Women's Waiting Room* **cultural programs** and other scheduled events.

Wallace, Idaho

Point of Interest: Portions of the 1980 movie *Heaven's Gate* were filmed on this street and *Dante's Peak* (1996) was filmed all over town. The set construction for *Heaven's Gate* kept up to 100 laborers busy for several months as Sixth Street was transformed into a historical western town complete with dirt streets. Despite disasterous reviews back in the 80s, *Heaven's Gate* went through a number of edits through the years and was re-released in 2012 to surprisingly favorable acclaim. The Northern Pacific Depot Museum has items from the sets of both movies in its collection.

Be part of the lively audience at **Sixth Street Melodrama** across the street from the museum. Cheering the heroes and jeering at the villains is part of the experience at the plays, many of which are original works inspired by local history and developed by people in the community. To see the show schedule and purchase tickets, go to sixthstreetmelodrama.com.

The **Silver Streak Zip Line Tours** welcome center is a half block west on Pine St. Zip line riders are transported from here up the mountain to three miles of cable on two courses. The western course has six runs, and the eastern course, four. Zip line rides are in high demand, so if you want to experience Idaho's biggest rush, review the policies about weight limits and health, make reservations, and pay in advance with a credit card at silverstreakziplinetours.com. If you drop in hoping for a spur of the moment ride, there may not be an opening.

If you are staying at the vintage **Stardust Motel**, keep going west on Pine, a half block past the spaceship on Fifth and Pine.

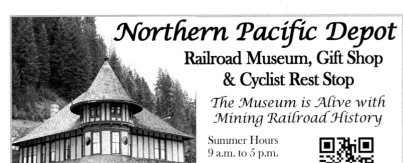

The **Stardust Motel** provides affordable vintage lodging in the heart of downtown Wallace. The spacious rooms include queen, and king size bed options. All rooms have coffee makers, fridges, and **free Wifi**. If you desire a microwave, request it when making your reservation. This is both a **pet-friendly** and cycle friendly establishment. Bicycles may be brought into rooms or locked to the railings. Guests are free to use the indoor **pool, hot tub, sauna, steamroom,** and **exercise room** at the Wallace Inn. If the Stardust office is closed upon arrival, please check in at the Wallace Inn.

Find tasty food and interesting décor at the **Red Light Garage**, just steps from the Stardust. They're famous for the hearty breakfast burrito, huckleberry waffles, and espresso. Owners Jamie and Barbara have expanded the menu to include a variety of 24 delectable hamburgers, "the best along I-90." **Vegetarians** can get a meatless garden burger. Or, choose from wraps, salads, sandwiches, and shakes, of which huckleberry is a favorite. Dine inside or enjoy your meal on the patio. Customers like to climb into the spaceship—technically a Korean weather satellite—for a souvenir photo.

The following description of Wallace traces a route east from the Brooks Hotel on Fifth and Cedar then south on Sixth to Bank. (The post office is on the block west of Cedar and Fifth).

Wallace, Idaho

The Red Light Garage with spaceship on Fifth and Pine

The chef statue on the corner of Fifth and Cedar welcomes you to the Brooks Hotel and Restaurant. The restaurant and lounge are open daily. For breakfast, they serve a variety of dishes, from granola and yogurt, to American fare that includes potatoes **grown in Idaho**. Prime rib is the specialty for dinner on Fri. and Sat. Choice meats are **cut locally** at the Wayside Market in Smelterville. Try a tantalizing **huckleberry dessert** when berries are in season, or purchase **fresh berries by the quart or gallon**. The hotel rooms are clean and affordable. If you require a fridge or microwave mention it when making reservations as not all rooms include them. Suites with **full kitchens** are upstairs (walk up). Bikes may be brought into the rooms or stored in the office over night. They rarely check email so you're better off to call. 208.556.1571.

Point of Interest: Mrs. Lucy A. Wallace came to join her husband in the spring of 1885. He met her at the Old Mission, where she arrived by steamboat with a dog, bird, cats, chickens, and all the necessary homemaking essentials. From there, they struggled through the mud by wagon, and crossed the river 14 times. The water was high and dangerous because of the melting snow. The second ford crossed a narrow channel with a rapid current and their wagon became wedged between two boulders about midstream. Col. Wallace walked out on the tongue of the wagon with an ax and leaped to shore, where he cut some saplings and used them to pry the wheels free. A chicken drowned at another crossing when water inundated the wagon. By winter of that year, Mrs. Wallace was one of only four women in the vicinity who were braving the rigors of the mining camp lifestyle.

Wallace, Idaho

The Metals Bar at 514 Cedar is open 10 a.m. to 2 a.m. daily. Relax and enjoy a cold brew, local **Northwest wines**, or cocktail in this neighborhood lounge with a mining theme. You are likely to meet locals here who have worked in the mines and can identify each one of the locations in the **mine photos** on the walls. As you rub shoulders with folks born and raised here, you will find they are a wealth of information about the area. Play a game of **darts, pool,** or **shuffleboard.** Help yourself to popcorn or munch on dill pickle pretzels (kept in buckets under the popcorn machine). This is one of Idaho's many smoking bars. They installed a state-of-the-art ventilation system for non-smoking guests, and it is amazingly effective. They often have **live music** on weekends. See updates about The Metals Bar on their Facebook page.

Point of Interest: Drinking alcoholic beverages has been a historically popular activity throughout the mining district from the start. It has provided a welcome distraction for those who work long hours under grueling conditions. And beer was the drink of choice when typhoid polluted local drinking water supplies. Some 200 saloons were flourishing in Shoshone County when Idaho signed up for Prohibition in 1916. Faced with the loss of their livelihoods, bar owners tried selling fruit juices, ginger ale, and soda water to their unhappy customers.

It quickly became evident that the anti-drinking law was not effective at diminishing the desire for booze, and the ever-resourceful Silver Valley entrepreneurs found ways to fill the demand. Black market alcohol seeped over the border from Montana by rail, pack train, and later, automobile. There was a general understanding that local sheriffs were expected to turn a blind eye. Meanwhile, clandestine stills multiplied in forests, cellars, and mines. Some people even acquired a taste for "silo juice," a fermented liquid that seeps to the bottom of silos. The resistance to Prohibition was known as the "North Idaho Whiskey Rebellion," and it resulted in a crackdown in the summer of 1929, as government agents swooped in and arrested nearly 200 drinkers, including the Shoshone County sheriff, deputy sheriff, assessor, city officials from Mullan and Wallace, and other prominent citizens.

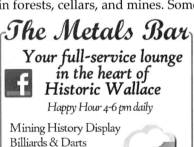

Wallace, Idaho

The Nook, across the street, is an intimate eatery that serves wraps, salads, and sandwiches on **fresh baked breads.** Everything is made from scratch. Open daily in summer, 11 a.m. to 9 p.m. The Nook delivers to the Wallace Inn, the Ryan, and The Banker. 208.556.5522. This is also where you will find the **Sam Brooks Wallace Laundromat,** with the antique wringer washer outside, open daily from 7 a.m. to 8 p.m.

6th and Cedar is a new coffee shop in the historic Wallace Corner building, serving **organic coffee** roasted locally at Silver Cup Coffee Roasters of Kellogg. The selection includes lattes, mochas, soy alternatives, tea, and baked goods. They open daily at 6 a.m. The building is being renovated and includes the studio of custom leather artisan, Ryder Gauteraux. The three shops you can see across the street on Cedar offer lots of vintage and second-hand browsing.

Point of Interest: This is the former **Red Light District** of Wallace. About a dozen brothels flanked the area around Sixth, Pine and Cedar Streets for a century. Some bawdy (body) houses were registered as female boarding homes. Others operated out of Wild West saloons, dance halls, and burlesque theaters. After the turn of the century, there was a campaign to move the *cribs* away from churches and schools in the residential area that was expanding west of Fifth St. A cluster of the houses remained east of Fifth on Pine, and others were relocated to where the NP Depot Museum is now. It was also the site of the Coliseum Theater, the largest of five burlesque halls in town., which featured a carousel stage. The Lux began operating on the northeast corner of Sixth and Cedar in 1977, one of a chain of brothels on the 600 block of

Window display at the Oasis Bordello Museum on Cedar St.

Wallace, Idaho

Cedar: The Lux, The Oasis, The Luxette, and the U&I Rooms.

The Lux is now a freshly renovated boutique hotel. The spacious Madame Suite includes private bath, mini-bar, fridge, and flat screen TV. The other rooms provide a retro lodging experience, which means no electronic contraptions except for the free Wifi. The main focus is the bed, and the birds eye view of downtown Wallace and surrounding hills. Most rooms have their own sinks. Tubs/showers are down the hall. Cycles can be locked up across the street inside the Hotel Ryan, which is owned by the same folks.

Rooms at the historic **Hotel Ryan** feature antique and vintage furnishings, free Wifi, and most have private baths. Most rooms have mini-fridges. Guests who desire a microwave need to request it when making reservations. Only the Owner's Suite has a TV. All rooms are accessed by stairs to the second level. The front door remains locked for privacy and security. The emphasis at both hotels is hospitality.

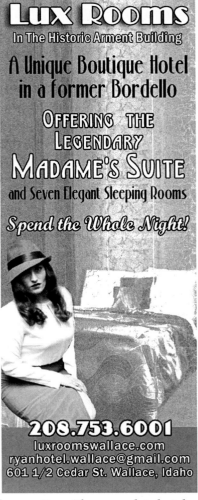

Rent a room or the whole place. When renting either complete hotel, a full kitchen becomes available. The Ryan also has a lounging area with TV and small kitchen. Inquire about **package deals** with the **Silver Streak Zip Line** and wine tasting at **The Fainting Goat**. 208.753.6001.

Take a **guided tour** of Wallace's famous **Oasis Bordello Museum** across from the Ryan. Get a glimpse at the everyday life of "working women" in this authentic brothel that closed in 1988. They open "around Memorial Day" to the end of September. Tours leave from the gift shop on the half hour. Admission $5. 208.753.0801

Wallace, Idaho

Heading south on Sixth St., you may feel yourself pulled by a mysterious force. That could be because you are approaching the **"Probablistic Center of the Universe,"** so dubbed by a former mayor of Wallace, as a challenge, more or less, to anyone who could disprove his assertion. When arriving at Sixth and Bank, you will see the **Center of the Universe** is a plaque at the intersection, that pays tribute to the central importance of mining in Idaho's Silver Valley, with stock symbols of the district's remaining mines decorating the perimeter. This year's book cover features cyclists Nancy and Mike Merickel of Washington state, who were circumnavigating the Center of the Universe—something they do whenever they come to Wallace. Some people get married here. Many just have their pictures taken.

The mouth-watering aroma wafting in the air comes from the smoker on the sidewalk outside the **Historic Smokehouse Barbecue & Saloon.** The Memphis style barbecue can be enjoyed inside or at one of the sidewalk tables. Special diets are accommodated too, with daily vegetable specials and **organic** spring mix salad. Go to **smokehousebbqsaloon.com** to see the menu. Relax and absorb the good vibes as you take in the view of classic Wallace architecture framed against the mountains that encircle the town.

The **Wallace District Mining Museum and Visitor Center** about half way down the block toward the west, is open seven days a week in summer. Stop in to learn about the Coeur d'Alene Mining District's many contributions to this region and the world.

Wallace, Idaho

There are scavenger hunts for the kids and a twenty-minute film called, *North Idaho's Silver Legacy.* Pay your respects to **The Last Stop Light** between Seattle and Boston, lying in state here. It hung at Seventh and Bank Streets when I-90 snaked through town. When highway improvements threatened demolition of the beautiful old buildings downtown, the citizens rescued Wallace by getting the entire business district listed on the National Register of Historic Places, and their victory was written up in major newspapers from coast to coast.

The museum gift shop has commemorative **silver medallions** and **local history books**. See mine models and exhibits that give visitors a "true mining experience." There is a **public restroom** here

Looking west on Bank Street toward the mining museum

and **visitor information** about regional attractions. Ask them about biking and hiking trails around Wallace, such as the **Pulaski Trail**. Museum admission is Adults $3/Kids $1. See wallacedistrictminingmuseum.org for special rates, events, and seasonal hours 208.556.1592.

The **Sierra Silver Mine** waiting room is on the corner of Fifth and Bank. Board a trolley for a ride to an underground mine tour to learn about hard rock mining. Open daily May 1 to Oct. 12, $15 adults/$8.50 kids. Tours leave every half hour. Or take the trolley to Burke and get a unique history lesson from a costumed guide. Wed. through Sat. in July and August, 11 to 3 p.m. $10 adults/$6 kids for the 50-minute tour.

Hike on the 3-mile Pulaski Trail on the outskirts of Wallace.

Wallace, Idaho

The Banker is a charming vacation home across from the mine tour. There is plenty of room for a family or group in the two-story home with three bedrooms, two bathrooms, living room with flat screen TV, Wifi, full kitchen with dishwasher, dining area, washer/dryer, and full basement for lots of secure cycle storage.

Two night minimum stay starts at $125 with discounts for additional nights. See interior pictures at kelloggvacationhomes.com/banker.html and call 800-435-2588 for reservations.

Step into some local history at the new **Wallace Stairs** interpretive signs across from the 'Silver Mine tour, and **"Hike the Stairs"** for a bird's eye view of Wallace. Hiking all twelve of Wallace's historic stairways is the equivalent of climbing a 46-story building! See a quick tour of the stairs hike here: youtu.be/SR-QDiI_HCA.

Browse the unique **North Idaho Trading Co**. pawn shop at the junction of Fifth and Bank. This is also the home of the non-profit **Historical Wallace Preservation Society** which has catalogued and digized thousands of **pictures** of mining, logging, and railroading history in and around Wallace and they can be purchased for a nominal fee.

The **Fainting Goat Wine Bar & Eatery** across from the mining museum serves nouvelle tapas cuisine and wines from around the world. Unique and seasonal combinations are arfully presented, and served with regional and international wine, beer and cider in a rustic chic setting, where the furnishings have been handcrafted by the owner from salvaged and upcycled materials. Wine can be ordered by the glass or purchased from the *Enomatic* wine dispenser. The Goat serves occasional gourmet dinners paired with wines. **Farm Girls Tea** next door offers a wide variety of loose leaf teas from around the world.

Wallace, Idaho

Continue east on Bank St. for shops, restaurants, microbrew tasting, groceries, and camping supplies. A detour south at the intersection of Sixth and Bank, leads to the city pool, open daily in summer.

Point of Interest: An opera house once stood where the pool is now, and as has often been the case in Wallace's colorful history, events that transpired there one night made headlines in far away cities around the nation.

Theatrical performances provided a welcome distraction from a hard life in what has been called one of America's most colorful and raucous frontier towns. Popular itinerant performers braved the rigors of travel to bring the refining influences of culture to rugged outposts like Wallace. Of course the advent of trains made hauling sets, costumes, and other accoutrements of the thespian's trade much easier than moving everything by wagon and boat, as had previously been the case.

One of the most popular productions to go on tour from New York City was Alexander Dumas' swashbuckling romance, *The Count of Monte Cristo*, with James O'Neill playing the lead role of Edmond Dantes. Eleven years into the show's successful 25-year tour schedule, it came to Wallace in 1904, where a pleasant evening at the theater was marred by an unfortunate shoot-out and subsequent stampede.

The problem started after William Cuff, a miner and US veteran who had fought in the Philippines, lit up a cigar in the theater's gallery, perhaps assuming his service to the country had earned him that right. But house policeman Rose figured differently and ordered Cuff to put it out. This led to a tussle wherein the officer grabbed the cigar, which further perturbed Cuff, who stormed off vowing vengeance. He returned shortly thereafter with a revolver and waited outside for the show to end. Rose was first to exit, with the theater goers close behind. Cuff fired at him and missed. The stray bullet struck a well-known surgeon, Dr. Fims, in the head and killed him instantly. At that, the theater patrons panicked and rushed back inside to find safety but some were trampled in the milieu. Cuff continued firing as police arrived, and he shot Chief McGovern in the hand. When Cuff ran around the building to escape, he was intercepted by Officer Quinn, who shot him dead. Headlines blared that Cuff paid the ultimate price for a smoke.

The bike rack outside the **1313 Club Historic Saloon & Grill** says "Welcome!" Get a delicious breakfast, lunch, or dinner at this cyclist-owned restaurant in one of Wallace's historic buildings. The Heller building has served as a hotel, bus depot, barbershop, and café.

Wallace, Idaho

Sidewalk Seating at the 1313 Club on Bank St.

Decorations in this eclectic eatery include a nest of hibernating killer bees (safely tucked in a glass case), swooping piper cub, and a flying albino beaver.

Mexican dishes, steak, buffalo, big salads, homemade soups, wraps, and **vegetarian** garden burgers are some menu choices. The **huckleberry salmon** burger combines a homemade berry sauce and grilled onions over a salmon patty, for that quintessential Northwest flavor. Pasta lovers appreciate the "**Build a Pasta Bowl**." Choose spaghetti, penne, or fettucini, topped with one of three sauces: Alfredo, zesty meat, or marinara.

Enjoy the selection of **regional wines** and **microbrews** from **Wallace Brewing**, while pondering the various theories of how the 1313 Club got its name. Try the award-winning Red Light Irish Red Ale, or the 1910 Black Lager, reminiscent of German dark beers, but without the bitterness. There is **free Wifi** here. Open 7 a.m., Mon. through Sat. Breakfast is available until 10:30 a.m. Check out the menu at 1313club.com.

To sample the rest of **Wallace Brewing's** eight local microbrews, step into the Orehouse tasting room next door, decorated with some famous Wallace relics, like foam boulders from the set of *Dante's Peak* and an old bicycle that played a heroic role in the 1910 fire

Beer tasting starts at $1 per sample with larger servings available. Play free pool, chess, and hard tipped darts. See sample mining cores and ores. Inquire about a **tour** of the microbrew operation. You can stock up on brew by getting a growler-full for the

Historic Saloon & Grill
Breakfast ~ Lunch ~ Dinner

BURGERS ● STEAKS ● MEXICAN
BUFFALO BURGERS
HOMEMADE SOUPS & DAILY SPECIALS

Go Slow & Hurry Back!

 OPEN MON - SAT
Closed Sun.

Cyclist Owned & Operated!

608 Bank St., Wallace, Idaho
208.752.9391 ~ 1313club.com

Wallace, Idaho

road. When you are in town during one of Wallace's popular street festivals, it's okay to wander around town with an open container, as long as it's a red solo cup. (Wallace lodgings fill up fast during those days, so check wallaceidahochamber.com for events and reserve early.)

Recapture the more refined features of days gone by with a tea break in **The Silver Tea Room** inside **Price Tag Antiques**. Select from a wide variety of iced or hot British teas and a menu of delights. Drop in for a pot of tea for one, or gather with new and old friends around an elegantly set table to enjoy a four-course luncheon tea, afternoon tea, or five-course full tea in this British-style tearoom without the stuffiness. You can also order soup and sandwich, salad and sandwich, or *al la cart* anytime. Tea is served between 11 a.m. and 4 p.m. Please make reservations in advance for parties of three or more by calling 208.556.1500.

Price Tag Antiques has more than 7,000 square feet of **high-end antiques and collectibles**. Victorian, American, and European pieces, primitives, western items, jewelry, toys, greeting cards, old books, art, **huckleberry and chocolate delights**, and vintage clothing, including fur coats. Have your **Old Time Photos** taken in costume. Dress up in hats as you sip tea, relax, shop, and visit with your friends. Summer hours are 10 a.m. to 6 p.m.

The Pizza Factory is down the block on the corner of Seventh and Bank, where the famous stoplight saw it's last days in 1993. Get back on the bike trail by returning to the trailhead on Sixth St., or you can catch the trail under the freeway across from **Harvest Foods**. The latter route also goes by **Wallace Hardware**, where you can get some basic emergency bike parts and camping gear.

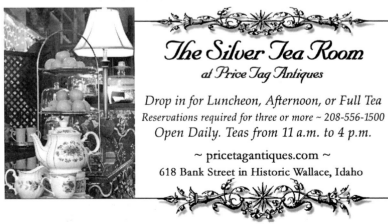

The Silver Tea Room
at Price Tag Antiques

Drop in for Luncheon, Afternoon, or Full Tea
Reservations required for three or more ~ 208-556-1500
Open Daily. Teas from 11 a.m. to 4 p.m.

~ pricetagantiques.com ~
618 Bank Street in Historic Wallace, Idaho

Restless Rapids Scenic Wayside

WHERE AM I? Trail Miles: 65.9
The South Fork Coeur d'Alene
River in eastern Shoshone
County.

REST STOP AMENITIES: Public
Restroom/Accessible, Picnic
Table, Interpretive Sign.
Next Stop: 1.8 miles

Golconda Scenic Wayside

WHERE AM I? Trail Miles: 67.7
The South Fork Coeur d'Alene
River in eastern Shoshone
County.

REST STOP AMENITIES: Picnic
Table, Interpretive Sign.
Next Stop: 3.7 miles.

Trail Miles: 71.4 Mullan Trailhead

DRIVING DIRECTIONS: Take
I-90 to Exit #68 to River St.
Trailhead is straight ahead.

TRAILHEAD AMENITIES:
Portable Toilet (seasonal), Pic-
nic Table, Interpretive Sign, 20
Parking Spaces/2 ADA. Room
for RVs. (Water, Food, Lodg-
ing, Camping, Museum,
Laundry, Post Office nearby)..
Next Stop: 7.1 miles.

Lucky Friday Mine Display, Mullan City Park

ELEVATION: 3,277 FT. **Mullan, Idaho**

Congratulations! You have pedaled across the entire State of Idaho (granted, it was the skinny part), from one end of the Trail of the Coeur d'Alenes to the other. You are in the City of Mullan, pop. 692, in the eastern portion of Shoshone County, six miles from Lookout Pass Ski Area and the Montana border.

The Mullan Trailhead marks the end of one trail and the point from which the Bitterroot Loop continues through the backwoods on the multi-use Northern Pacific Trail (Nor-Pac) to Lookout Pass and beyond to the Route of the Hiawatha, (RoH).

Lookout Motel, opposite the trailhead, has tiny, clean, and **very low-cost rooms** with mini-fridges and TVs. Ride two blocks north on Second St. to Earle to a statue of John Mullan on the left. The City Hall here provides **visitor information** during business hours.

Earle's Pub & Grub on the corner of Second and Earle is under new ownership once again, and serving breakfast, lunch, and dinner.

Mullan, Idaho

Call for updated hours 208. 744.7000. There is a tidy **public laundry** facility with change machine and soap dispenser in the building behind the lounge and a clean **public restroom.**

Across the street are the **city park**, **post office**, and **Captain John Mullan Museum**. The volunteer-run museum traces the history of Mullan with many artifacts donated by local families. See an old moonshine still and a detailed model of the steamboat *Idaho*. Learn about the building of the Mullan Mili-

The Captain John Mullan Museum opens weekdays in summer

tary Road. The historic newspapers are of interest to genealogical researchers, with a scanner and copy machine on site to aid the effort. Open weekdays, June through August, 10 a.m. to 4 p.m. or by appointment. Admission is by donation.

The place with the red patio shades across from the museum is **The Silver Shaft**, a comfortable family-stye restaurant that offers healthy housemade meals amidst pictures and memorabilia that honor miners past and present. They have 13 types of burgers named

Mullan, Idaho

after local mines and an amazing **selection of salads**, like **organic** fresh peach and grilled chicken, huckleberry with grilled salmon, or pepperoni and parmesan, just to name a few. Also on the menu are pizza and toasted sub sandwiches, pasta dishes, and chicken, pork, beef, fish, and seafood entrees. Look for the daily pie and soup choices on the blackboard under the dessert counter. **Vegan** and **vegetarian** meals, and **gluten-free** and sprouted grain breads are available. People with other special dietary needs are encouraged to make requests and the cook will attempt to accommodate those as well. Breakfast, lunch, and dinner are served all day. The **Wifi** works well and there are plenty of plugs to recharge your devices. When the weather is nice, you may find *One Gun & the Long Shots* performing live music on the patio. They play for donations and give the money to people in need, so please be generous with your contributions. Reservations are not required, but if traveling with a group it helps to call ahead: 208.512.0813.

Mullan House B&B at 501 Hunter caters to outdoor enthusiasts. You will be greeted with a complimentary glass of wine at this kid-friendly B&B with six beautifully decorated rooms, that have private baths, TVs, and Wifi. There is secure storage for bikes and a cleaning room. Guests have use of full kitchen and laundry. See more at mullanhouse.com.

To ride the next leg of the Bitterroot Loop, find the Northern Pacific Trail (Nor-Pac) sign on the east end of the Trail of the Coeur d'Alenes Mullan Trailhead. Keep an eye out for these markers, because they guide you through the woods to Lookout Pass and beyond to the I-90 Taft Exit #5 in Montana.

Begin the trip by crossing 3rd St. and ride east on Fisher, behind the big brick Athletic Pavilion on the left, until you meet Earle Street. Straight ahead on the right is **Mullan Trail**, a brand new trailside amenity with **cabins** for rent, **RV sites**, and a **convenience store**. The store opens at 4 a.m., so it is a handy place to stock up on items you will need for the the remote sections of trail coming up in the national forests.

Mullan, Idaho

After .2 mile on Earle St., slip onto BL-90. You will temporarily leave the Nor-Pac here as it crosses private land. Ride east on BL-90 (Friday Avenue), past the ball park, the interchange, and Lucky Friday mine. See a sign to Larson Rd. 1.5 miles from the trailhead. Get on Larson Road toward Shoshone Park and Hale Fish Hatchery. There is an old dairy at Larson, then another fork at 3.1 miles. Go left .2 mile towards **Shoshone Park,** where there are **public restrooms**, picnic tables, barbecue grills, and **drinking water**. This day use area is open 6 a.m. to 10 p.m. Hale Fish Hatchery is .3 mile past Shoshone Park. Buy a handful of fish food from the dispenser and **feed the fish**. Go left at the end of the pavement through a little cedar grove. At 3.9 miles, look for the Nor-Pac marker and bear right onto NF-3026 to get back on the multi-use Nor-Pac trail. At mile 5 go under I-90, then ride uphill to Stevens Lake Wayside stop.

Trail Miles: 78.5 Stevens Lake Wayside

WHERE AM I?
You are on NF Rd. 3026 near the trailhead to Stevens Peak in western Shoshone County.

REST STOP AMENITIES: Restroom, Picnic Table, Interpretive Sign, Hiking Trails.
Next Stop: .6 miles

Point of Interest: Stevens Peak (6,838) is the highest mountain in the western reaches of the Bitterroot range. It is a popular destination for climbing, hiking, and back country skiing. Inland Northwest groups often use it for mountaineering training.

After the wayside stop, turn left uphill at the switchback and look for the Nor-Pac sign on the left. Note, the Idaho Centenial Trail and Stevens Lake trail intersect at the hairpin, where they head south. Willow Creek Rd. also connects here and loops back to Mullan.

Trail Miles: 79.1 Dorsey Trailhead

DRIVING DIRECTIONS: There is no parking at this trailhead.

TRAILHEAD AMENITIES:
Interpretive Sign,
Next Stop: 3.2 miles

Point of Interest: Remnants of an old watering station can be seen on the right. This is where trains refilled water tanks so they didn't run out of steam when chugging over the pass.

ELEVATION: 4,738 FT. Trail Miles: 82.3 Lookout Pass Trailhead

DRIVING DIRECTIONS: Take I-90 to Exit #0. Lookout Pass parking lot is on the south side of the freeway.

TRAILHEAD AMENITIES: Interpretive Sign. (Parking, Restroom, Water, Trail Info, Hiking, Food, Camping, Rentals, Hiawatha Tickets nearby at the lodge).
Next Stop: 11.1 miles

Looking west from Lookout Pass

Lookout Pass Ski & Recreation Area serves as headquarters and visitor center for the Route of the Hiawatha. The lodge is open when the Hiawatha is, from the last weekend of May to the first weekend in October, weather permitting. The lodge has a **bike rental and repair shop,** (bike rack comes w/rental) **restrooms, gift shop, deli & grill** with **hamburgers, sandwiches** and **wraps, beer.** Mountain bikes or hybrids are recommended on the Hiawatha. Make sure everyone in your party has an emergency repair kit with extra tubes. Children under 14 must be with an adult. Helmets and lights are required on the Route of the Hiawatha. Stock up on plenty of **water** and food here as well.

There are several ways to **buy tickets** for the Hiawatha: at the lodge, online at skilookout.com/hiawatha, and from marshals on the trail (who

only accept cash). Tickets are also sold at Scheffy's store in Avery and at the Wallace Inn: $10 adult/$6 child. Six and under are free. If you plan to take the **bus** back up the RoH, pay the $9/$6 when purchasing tickets. There is **free camping** overnight in the Lookout Pass Ski Hill parking lot for self-contained RVs. Call 208.744.1301 or check ridethehiawatha.com.

To reach the Hiawatha, pick up the Nor-Pac trail on the east end of the parking area. You have crossed into Montana's Mineral County and the **Lolo National Forest**. (You have also crossed into the Mountain Time Zone). You will now be riding in the Superior Ranger District of the Lolo National Forest. Check for updates on

Copper Lake Trail, Lolo National Forest, in Montana

rules and conditions at fs.usda.gov/alerts/lolo/alerts-notices.

The St. Regis basin opens up before you after .5 mile. Stay left at the fork. There will be a hairpin turn after another .5 mile, and a **hiking/mountain bike trail** to lower St. Regis Lake and some primitive campsites. Another hiking/biking trail leads into the Copper Lake area a mile later. Within two miles, there is a dark and bumpy tunnel. Then you will go under I-90 twice. A half-mile later the trail meets a paved road (Bullion Cr. Rd/NF-507). This is Taft Exit #5 at I-90. Elevation, 3,630 ft.

Go straight until you see the **Route of the Hiawatha sign** to East Portal, Roland, and Pearson Trailheads. You are about 20.5 miles past the Mullan Trailhead. Take Rainey Creek Rd/ NF-506 up to the East Portal turnoff. It's about a 2% grade for 2 miles to the East Portal Trailhead.

If you're ready for a break, the nearest lodgings and supplies are 4.2 miles east at **Mangold's General Store and Motel** in Saltese, Montana. You can continue on the multi-use Nor-Pac Rd. and turn left under the I-90 underpass after 4 miles; or, pedal up to the East Portal Trailhead and catch the new **Route of the Olympian** to Saltese from the

Mangold's in Saltese, MT

northeast corner of the parking lot. The Olympian is non-motorized between here and Saltese from Memorial Day through Labor Day.

Point of Interest: Taft, "The wickedest city in America," blossomed here in 1907, when workers for the Chicago Milwaukee and St. Paul Railroad were blasting and digging the 1.7 mile long tunnel through St. Paul Pass. With 27 saloons and 750 men who toiled in extreme conditions, the town was a magnet for drinkers, gamblers, and prostitutes who were referred to as "canaries." Taft died out when the tunnel was finished, and its remains burned to the ground in the 1910 inferno.

Elevation: 4,147 FT. **Trail Miles: 93.4** East Portal Trailhead

DRIVING DIRECTIONS: Take I-90 to the Taft Exit #5 in Montana. Turn left to the Route of the Hiawatha sign. Turn right over the bridge onto NF-506. Drive two miles and turn left on the East Portal cut-off.

TRAILHEAD AMENITIES: Restrooms, Picnic Tables, Interpretive Signs, Route of the Hiawatha and Olympian Trail Access.
Next Stop: 1.9 miles

The 15-mile **Route of the Hiawatha** is in the Rails-to-Trails Conservancy Hall of Fame. It leads gently down a 1.7% grade on the abandoned Milwaukee Road railbed, traversing through ten **tunnels** and seven sky-high **trestles**. **Interpretive signs** tell about the building of the railroad in this rugged terrain. This non-motorized trail complies with ADA rules for dogs, motorized wheelchairs, and Other Power Driven Mobility Devices (OPDMDs).

The ride begins at the eastern entrance of the cool, drippy, and pitch black 1.7-mile Taft Tunnel, which cuts through the St. Paul Pass from Montana to Idaho. After riding a short way, the tunnel bends and you will be able to see a tiny but comforting point of light on the other end. Stay in your lane to the right, but keep away from the edges to avoid falling into the ditches that drain water from the tunnel.

Half way through the tunnel you cross over to the Idaho Panhandle National Forest. You'll be engaging in a bit of time travel as well, since it's Mountain time at the East Portal in Montana and Pacific Time in Idaho.

Those who prefer to forego the long dark tunnnel can bypass it and pick up the trail at Roland Trailhead on the other side of the pass. Cycle travelers will encounter an extremely steep 1.9-mile ride to Roland Summit (elevation: 5,180) on NF-506. At the top, the 506 crosses State Line Road back to Idaho. It's 3.9 miles downhill from there to the other end of the Taft Tunnel. Now you're on a 3-mile multi-use portion of the trail, so expect an occasional vehicle, particularly the buses that shuttle people and bikes up the mountain from Pearson Trailhead.

Roland Trailhead   Trail Miles: 95.3   Elevation: 4150 FT.

DRIVING DIRECTIONS: Take I-90 to the Taft Exit #5 in Montana. Turn left to the Route of the Hiawatha sign. Turn right over the bridge onto NF-506. Drive 7.5 miles over the pass to Roland Trailhead.

TRAILHEAD AMENITIES: Restrooms, Picnic Tables, Interpretive Sign, Parking, Shuttle Bus Stop. **Next Stop: 4.8 miles**

Point of Interest: When gazing out at the vast wilderness, it's hard to believe lively settlements once dotted the tracks between Taft and Avery. Roland had a two-story train depot, several large bunkhouses, and even a ski hill. Goups came by train from Spokane, Coeur d'Alene, Missoula, and Avery to enjoy a day on the slopes.

The waterfall outside the tunnel feeds Cliff Creek, which tumbles down to meet Loop Creek. The remote settlements of Grand Forks and Falcon mushroomed where the creeks converge on the valley floor. Falcon had a small store, post office, a forest ranger station, and even a jewelry store. Grand Forks was a Wild West town with 15 saloons and a slew of "sporting" women. It also housed the Bitterroot Mercantile and a small emergency hospital. Forest service officials were on a constant campaign to eradicate alcohol sales from the town, but the commodity was in great demand and they only succeeded in driving sales underground.

Elevation: 3.707 FT.   **Trail Miles: 100.1** **Adair Trailhead**

DRIVING DIRECTIONS: Take I-90 to Wallace Exit #61 and turn left on I-90 Business Loop. Turn right on Fifth St. and right on Cedar St., left on First St., and right on Bank St. This turns into NF-456 (Moon Pass Rd.) The pavement ends after about a mile. At about 18 miles turn left onto Loop Creek Rd/ NF-326 to the Adair Trailhead.

ALTERNATE DRIVING DIRECTIONS: Take I-90 to the Rose Lake Exit #34 on the eastern side of 4th of July Pass. Drive 32 miles on SR-3 to NF-50 (St. Joe River Rd.). Continue 47 miles to Avery and turn left onto NF-456 (Moon Pass Rd.). Go past the Pearson Trailhead .4 mile, then turn right onto Loop Creek Rd/NF-326 to Adair Trailhead.

TRAILHEAD AMENITIES: Parking, Restrooms, Interpretive Sign
Next Stop: 8.5 miles

Elevation; 3,175 FT.   **Trail Miles: 108.6** **Pearson Trailhead**

Riders wait to board a bus at Pearson Trailhead, bound for Roland Trailhead

DRIVING DIRECTIONS: I-90 to Wallace Exit #61, turn left on the I-90 Business Loop. Turn right on Fifth St. and right on Cedar St., left on First St., and right on Bank St. This turns into NF-456 (Moon Pass Rd.) The pavement ends after about a mile. At 18.5 miles you will see a Route of the Hiawatha sign. Turn to access Pearson Trailhead, which is .5 mile up the road.

ALTERNATE DRIVING DIRECTIONS: Take I-90 to the Rose Lake Exit #34 on the eastern side of 4th of July Pass. Drive 32 miles on SR-3 to NF-50 (St. Joe River Rd.). Continue 47 miles to Avery and turn left onto NF-456 (Moon Pass Rd.). It's 9 miles to the Pearson Trailhead.

TRAILHEAD AMENITIES: Parking, Restrooms, Picnic Tables, Interpretive Sign, Shuttle Bus back to Roland Trailhead. (Primitive camping nearby).
Next Stop: 10.8 miles

THE BITTERROOT LOOP
Route of the Hiawatha

Point of Interest: The partying and drinking Kelly brothers were sent to the Wild West by their father so they could become men after graduating from Yale. They settled in a mansion up the canyon across from Avery with two Japanese servants, and they opened Bitterroot Mercantile Company stores in Taft, Grand Forks, and Avery. Their home was the only one around Avery to burn in the 1910 Fire.

Many cyclists ride down from the Taft Tunnel then catch the **shuttle bus** back up the mountain at Pearson Trailhead. Leave the Taft Tunnel by noon if you want to take your time and not worry about missing the bus. Bus service times are reduced in September, so check the schedule when making plans.

You can arrange to be picked up at Pearson if you book a tour with **ROW Adventures**, based in Coeur d'Alene. **ROW** offers full day bike **tours** on the Hiawatha that include equipment, safety tips, transport to and from Coeur d'Alene, and a trailside picnic. Those who want to pedal back uphill can get picked up there by ROW as well. The minimum tour group size is six and maximum is 30. Find information at rowadventurecenter.com/adventures/Hiawatha-Trail-Bike-Tour.

Many cyclists who pedal up the gentle 1.7% instead of taking the shuttle, prefer to park at Pearson and ride uphill first, then reward themselves with a nice relaxing downhill ride. Those who say the 15-mile experience is over too quickly and wish the trail was longer, can find some ideas here to extend the fun a few more days.

There is free **dispersed (primitive) camping** near Pearson Trailhead along Loop Creek. To camp there, go down the trailhead access road, turn right (north) on Moon Pass Rd./NF-456, and ride .4 mile to Loop Creek Rd/NF-326. Turn right toward Moss Creek and Roland. Watch for the shuttle buses and other traffic. If you've paid to get on the shuttle bus, you can ask to be dropped off at the camping area. Shovels and five gallons of water are required for campfires at undeveloped sites in the forest. For forest alerts and updates in Idaho see fs.usda.gov/alerts/ipnf/alerts-notices, or call 208.245.4517.

The nearest outpost of **civilization** is Avery, Idaho, nine miles from Pearson Trailhead by way of Moon Pass Rd. Two routes lead to Avery from Pearson Trailhead: the Old Milwaukee Scenic/Alternate Route and Moon Pass Rd., and both follow the North Fork of the St. Joe on opposite sides of the river. The Old Milwaukee route is the recommended path laid out by the Friends of the Coeur d'Alene Trails as part of the Bitterroot Loop. It's 1.8-miles longer and the road is a bit rougher, but it's also closer to the river and less travelled by vehicles. To take the Milwaukee Rd. from Pearson Trailhead, exit down the access road and turn right onto Moon Pass Rd. Turn left at .4 mile, and take the bridge across the North Fork of the St. Joe River, then turn left again onto the Milwaukee route/Rd-1997, a single lane gravel road with pullouts. Another road called NF-1997 intersects two miles down the road and leads to the Arid Peak fire lookout. At 5.6 miles you will see a trestle over the river. Telichpah Campground is .5 mile farther.

Tunnel on the Moon Pass Rd.

The historical USFS **Arid Peak Lookout** across from Loop Creek and the RoH was built at 5,306 feet high in 1934 to help detect fires, especially those sparked by the Milwaukee Railroad. Rental of the 20-foot high fire lookout starts at $25/night. Features include two cots with mattresses, dishes, propane lantern, propane camp stove, water containers, replica fire finder, wood stove, and 360 degree views. You supply the bedding and propane. Water must be hauled in or fetched from a stream and treated. There is an outhouse nearby. To find Arid Peak go right from the Pearson Trailhead access road, then left to the bridge .4 mile later on Moon Pass Rd.

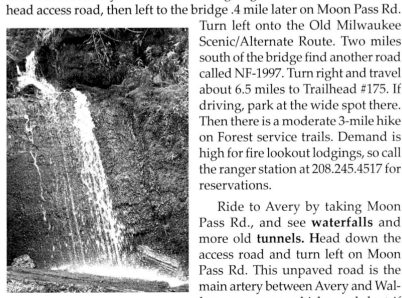

Turn left onto the Old Milwaukee Scenic/Alternate Route. Two miles south of the bridge find another road called NF-1997. Turn right and travel about 6.5 miles to Trailhead #175. If driving, park at the wide spot there. Then there is a moderate 3-mile hike on Forest service trails. Demand is high for fire lookout lodgings, so call the ranger station at 208.245.4517 for reservations.

Ride to Avery by taking Moon Pass Rd., and see **waterfalls** and more old **tunnels.** Head down the access road and turn left on Moon Pass Rd. This unpaved road is the main artery between Avery and Wallace, so expect vehicles and dust if

Waterfall along Moon Pass Rd. to Avery

Avery, Idaho

the weather is dry. After 5 miles cross a bridge over the North Fork of the St. Joe River. Continue to Avery on Moon Pass Rd., or to camp by the river, turn right after the bridge, ride downhill and turn right again on the Old Milwaukee Rd. It's .5 mile to Telichpah campground.

Telichpah Campground on the North Fork of the St. Joe River has 5 small camping units with fireplaces or grills and picnic tables, but no drinking water. **Restrooms** are vault toilets and trash must be packed out. Trailers are not recommended. This is a trailhead for the Nelson Peak National Recreation Trail System. **Hike** and **mountain bike** on Telichpah Creek Trail #196, which connects to Nelson Ridge Trail #186. Camping is free on a first-come-first-served basis. Call the St. Joe Ranger District, 208.245.2531. You are in bear country so keep a clean and odor-free camp. Get all kinds of bear information at bebearaware.org.

The Milwaukee route continues from the south end of the campground and the road gets rougher on this stretch. It's 4.5 more miles to the paved St. Joe River Rd./NF-50, where you turn right and ride another .1 mile into Avery.

Avery, Idaho   Trail Miles: 119.4   ELEVATION: 2,440 FT.

DRIVING DIRECTIONS: If coming from east of 4th of July Pass: take I-90 to the Rose Lake Exit #34. Drive south 32 miles on Hwy 3 to NF-50 (St. Joe River Rd.). Turn left and continue 47 miles to Avery.

ALTERNATE DRIVING DIRECTIONS: From Spokane: take I-90 Sandpoint/Moscow exit to Hwy 95 south and drive 31 miles to Plummer. Turn left on SR-5 and go 18 miles to St. Maries. Follow the road to the east end of downtown. Immediately after the curve with the Logger Memorial, turn left and go one block to the four-way stop, then left again over the St. Joe River bridge. Drive .6 mile, and turn right onto St. Joe River Rd.NF-50. Follow the river 47 miles to Avery.

AMENITIES: Restroom (open during business hrs.), Lodging, Shopping, Museum, Post Office, Roadside Attractions. (Camping, Showers, Laundry, Water, Food, Phones nearby). **Next Stop: 12.8 miles.**

Avery, Idaho, (pop. 50, more or less) is nestled in the St. Joe River valley, surrounded by thousands of acres of forested wilderness. Once a busy railroad stop and logging town, Avery is a year-round base camp for kayakers, fishermen, hunters, hikers, and snowmobilers. It's the place

Avery, Idaho

to rest up before continuing toward St. Maries. Find lodgings, a hot shower, supplies, and a bite to eat. There is no cell service here. With more than 100 miles of free-flowing river, "The Joe" offers a variety of experiences from a gentle float, to hardcore **Class IV and V rapids**. See what rafting on The Joe looks like at rowadventures.com

Look for **Scheffy's Motel** and **convenience store** when heading west along the St. Joe River Rd. The motel rooms sleep up to six and include full kitchens. Guests can make free long distance phone calls on the land line. The public may use the **bathhouse** for $6. It has both **tubs and showers**. Add $2 if you need a towel. There is also a coin-op **laundry**. Get **tickets** to the Route of the Hiawatha in the store.

The **Idaho Fly Fishing Company** is across the road. Get outfitted for fly fishing and meet the owner, Dan, an avid road cyclist. He pedaled across the U.S. last year and enjoys sharing his story with fellow riders. Find coffee service inside with deli-style sandwiches, hard ice cream, and shakes, with huckleberry being the most popular. Open daily 8 a.m. to 6 p.m. Memorial Day to Labor Day. 208.245.3626.

In the heart of Avery, you will find a **gift shop** and several **roadside attractions** such as the old **Milwaukee Road dining car, historical museum, jail** and **trout pond**. The **public restroom** and museum are open during post office hours. The trout pond is a favorite stop. Buy a handful of fish food for 25 cents and watch them eat.

There is a modern vacation rental above the gift shop in this Old West style building across from Avery's roadside attractions

Avery Gift Shop is across the street from the roadside attractions. Stop in for **huckleberry** treats, local crafts, and **souvenirs** with hunting, railroad, and Avery themes. Relax outside at the picnic table or around the fire pit. A modern and reasonably priced **vacation suite** above the gift shop sleeps eight. There is a bedroom with two queen beds, another with two twins, and room for two more on the sofa sleeper in the living room. The lodgings include **satellite TV, air conditioning,** and **free local phone service**. Make sure to have a calling card in your survival kit. The kitchen is stocked with dishes, utensils, pots and

Avery , Idaho

pans—everything but the food. See averygiftshop.com for reservations, or 208.245.1308, and 208.245.2055 after hours.

If you are staying at **Cabins By The Joe & RV Park,** head west from the Avery Gift Shop on Siberts Old River Rd. It's a .5 mile ride over the bridge, past the old Avery school and along the river to the cabins.

Cabins by The Joe overlook the St. Joe River and include full bathrooms, linens, memory foam and pillow-top mattresses, microwave, fridge, air conditioning, satellite TV and coffee maker. Two cabins have

kitchens stocked with cookware. Waterfront RV Sites include full hookups with water, 30 and 50 amp power, and sewer. See the nightly and extended stay rates, and photos at cabinsbythejoe.com, or call 425.773.3724 for reservations.

Cabins by the Joe, on the south side of the St. Joe River

Point of Interest: The little railroad and logging town of Avery is probably the last place you would expect people to throw a big bash for the Japanese emperor's birthday. However, the annual party was a popular event in Avery's history, after nearly 80 Japanese settled here to help build the Milwaukee Road. Railroad owners, like the Rockefellers of Standard Oil, and Phillip Armour of Armour Meat packing interests, were looking to get into the lucrative Japanese silk trade, and to get a foothold, railroad executives promised to hire Japanese construction laborers in exchange for access to Japanese markets. The workers who settled in Avery decided to show their appreciation to their new community by throwing a party on the emperor's birthday. Local Japanese community, leader, Ben Goto, supplied food, liquor, candies, and gifts for the guests—such as embroidered slippers for all. A great deal of booze flowed during this celebration and a handcart stood by to haul home those who overindulged. The Japanese community persisted in Avery until the 1950s. Some displaced during World War II sought refuge with relatives here, and children who had been in the concentration camps later attended school in Avery.

Do you want to continue on the unpaved multi-use route laid out by the Friends of the Coeur d'Alene Trails group, or would you prefer to cruise the 47 miles to St. Maries on the paved St. Joe River Rd/NF-50?

Avery , Idaho

The paved road is faster, less dusty, and has more amenities, but you will be competing for road space with log trucks and recreational vehicles pulling trailers. The lack of decent shoulders results in less than ideal riding conditions, mainly because the average rural north Idaho driver, who has no problem attempting to dodge deer, moose, dogs, and various birds in the road on a regular basis, finds it unusual to slow down for, or go around, cyclists. That said, the chart at right shows distances to amenities on the St. Joe River Rd. between Avery and St. Maries. Those following the route prescribed by the Friends group will still be able to reach these services from an occasional bridge or access road and biking a few extra miles.

ST. JOE RIVER RD. Avery to St. Maries	
Avery	0
Vault Toilet Restroom	1.2
USFS Ranger Station	6.0
Marble Creek Day Use	12.2
St. Joe Lodge	12.8
Spring Creek Cabins	14.3
BLM Huckleberry Campground	16.5
Calder Store Turn Off	22.4
Big Eddy Hotel/ Campground & Rest-Bar	27.6
Shadowy St. Joe Campground	37
St. Maries	47

Siberts Old River Rd, turns to packed gravel just beyond Cabins by the Joe. There is a pedestrian bridge 5.9 miles after the cabins, which leads to the Avery Ranger Station (208.245.4517). There is **visitor information** and a **public restroom** here. Back on the trail, stay along the river. You will come out at the St. Joe River Rd. 12.8 miles past Avery. Turn left for the Marble Creek Interpretive Center (.2 mile away).

Trail Miles: 132.2 Marble Creek Interpretive Center
ELEVATION: 2,280 FT.

DRIVING DIRECTIONS: See directions for Avery, Idaho. Marble Creek is 34 miles up NF-50 (The St. Joe River Rd.).

AMENITIES: Restroom/Accessible, Water, Picnic Tables, Interpretive Displays, Parking, Swimming **Next Stop: 9.5 miles**

See **historical photos** and **artifacts**, and read about early 20th century logging methods. The interpretive center is a gateway to historic Marble Creek. A dirt road leads south to 60 miles of backcountry mountain trails and relics of the area's logging legacy, including homestead cabins, steam donkey engines, and the Hobo Cedar Grove hiking trail. This rest stop is for day use only, and it is a popular spot for river floaters to put their tubes and rafts in.

Point of Interest: Outlaws found the rough and remote wilderness south of the St. Joe River to be a good place to hide out. When Wyatt Earp and his brothers were running the White Elephant saloon in the gold-crazed settlement of Eagle City up the North Fork of the Coeur d'Alene River, a gunfight ensued over ownership of a town lot. The fight involved a character named William Buzzard, who found it necessary to go on the run. There are stories of him hiding south of here, at a place called Buzzard's Roost near Outlaw Ridge.

Turn west out of the parking lot onto St. Joe River Rd/NF-50, and take a right .25 mile over the wood plank bridge to the north side of the river. Make a left onto Potlatch Rd., the Old Milwaukee right of way, and follow the sign toward Big Creek and Calder.

Wooden Plank Bridge over The St. Joe River near Marble Creek.

Watch for moose, eagle, and other wildlife in the wetlands along the river. At 4.6 miles you come to the 515-foot Herrick Tunnel (No. 37). There is a nice turnout at the entrance to pull over and enjoy the view. Look for Big Creek Bridge 1.2 miles past the tunnel. The town of Herrick was to the right. Ride another 4 miles to Calder.

If you want **food** and **lodgings** at **St. Joe Lodge**, ride .6 miles past Marble Creek on the St. Joe River Rd./NF-50. They serve lunch and dinner, and co-owner Lynnel says the menu "changes a lot." There are two **bedrooms** for $50/night: one sleeps two, the other four. The shared bath has a clawfoot tub. She will cook breakfast on request for lodging guests for an additional charge. Play a game of shuffle board and hang out around the riverside fire pit. Get a sandwich and water for the remote section of trail ahead. Make reservations at 208.245.2284.

The Herrick Tunnel on the Old Milwaukee Rd.

Spring Creek Cabins are 2 miles past Marble Creek on the St. Joe River Rd. They can accommodate twenty people. Bathing facilities are in the community shower house. There is a **public telephone** here for use with your calling card. **Huckleberry Camground** is 4.3 miles past Marble Creek at MP 32. Go 6 more miles to the Calder turn-off.

ELEVATION: 2,240 FT. **Trail Miles: 141.7** **Calder, Idaho**

DRIVING DIRECTIONS: See directions for Avery, Idaho. The Calder turnoff is 23.3 miles up The St. Joe River Rd./NF-50.

AMENITIES: Restroom, Water, Picnic Area, Parking, Camping, Food, Post Office.
Next Stop: 24 miles

Calder Store is a combination restaurant, lounge, and small **convenience store** open daily in summer. Get scoop ice cream, drinks, AA batteries, chocolate bars, firewood, and camping food like hot dogs and marshmallows. Arrive at the restaurant before noon to order a hearty breakfast such as **huckleberry pancakes** and eggs. They serve good home-cooked dinners. There is **free tent camping** in the grassy area out back. No tent? No problem. Request one of the loaners.

Three-fourths of a mile down the trail from Calder is a weak link on this loop in the form of a bridge with cement baricades due to fire damage. Some people walk their bikes across the charred timbers. (Also, you may encounter large puddles for a few miles past the bridge). An alternative is to get on the paved St. Joe River Rd/NF-50 at Calder and ride 7.7 miles to reconnect with the Potlatch Rd./Milwaukee route. Either that, or follow this circuitous up and down detour, also explained on the Friends of the Coeur

The author checks the burned out bridge near Calder

d'Alenes Trails Web site. From Calder Store, turn right, then immediately left onto First St. Cross a cattle guard. It's flat for about a mile, then there is a hairpin left turn uphill. After 4 miles there is a sharp left turnoff that leads back down to Potlatch Rd.

After 3.6 miles on you will pass under the St. Joe River Rd. and come to a fork. Stay left and ride over the trestle bridge. After another 3 miles you will come to the junction of St. Joe City Rd. and Potlatch Rd. Today, this is just a quiet backwoods intersection, but back in the day, two rollicking frontier towns flourished here.

To stay on the Old Milwaukee Rd. (Potlatch Rd.) bear left and ride over the trestle over the St. Joe River. The road on the right leads back to the paved St. Joe River Rd.

Point of Interest: St Joe City marks the head of navigation on the highest navigable river in the world. The town of Ferrell boomed to 1,000 people on the north side of the river in the late 1880s when the logging boom was in full swing. The river was a frenzied lane of travel then, with logs floating down and steamboats full of fortune hunters, gamblers, lumber barons, sightseers, and settlers riding up. Ferrell had hotels, stores, a theater, bank, floating hospital, and saloons with "houses" upstairs, where over 30 prostitutes parted men from their hard-earned pay. But when the railroad laid its tracks on the south side of the river, a new town called St. Joe City sprang up around the depot and Ferrell died on the vine. The film, *The Tornado,* was filmed in St. Joe City in 1925. There are no vistor amenities there now.

If you can't make it to St. Maries and are prepared for **camping,** turn right on St. Joe City Rd., go .7 mile, then left on the St. Joe River Rd./NF-50 and 2.2 miles to the USFS Shadowy St. Joe Campground. It has vault **toilets, drinking water, firewood** for sale, and a host. There are no showers but you can take a dip in the river. 208.245.4517.

Back on the trail, Potlatch Rd. turns into Railroad Grade Rd. east of the St. Joe City Rd. junction. After 11 miles, you'll cross railroad tracks and come out on the paved Milwaukee Rd. Turn right (west) .8 mile to State Route 3 (SR-3), the *White Pine Scenic Byway.* After 165 miles on the Bitterroot Loop, you will now switch from dedicated and multi-use trails to state highway riding. Downtown St. Maries and lodging options are to the right, across the bridge over the St. Maries River.

ELEVATION: 2,127 FT. **Trail Miles: 165.7** ## St. Maries, Idaho

DRIVING DIRECTIONS: If coming from east of 4th of July Pass: take I-90 to the Rose Lake Exit #34. Drive south 32.7 miles on SR-3 to St. Maries.

From Spokane: On I-90 take Sandpoint/ Moscow exit to Hwy 95 south and drive 31 miles to Plummer. Turn left on SR-5 and drive 18 miles to St. Maries.

AMENITIES: (Restroom, Water, Picnic Area, Interpretive Signs, Food, Lodging, Camping, Swimming, Shopping, Museum, Mural Tour, Rentals, Laundry, Post Office nearby). **Next Stop: 12 miles**.

Logger Memorial,
St. Maries, Idaho

St. Maries, (pronounced *Mary's*) pop. 2,333, at the confluence of the St. Joe and St. Maries Rivers, is the Benewah County seat, and the largest city in the county.

The remainder of the Loop goes through downtown St. Maries, then west to Heyburn Park on SR-5, a winding two-lane commuter route with narrow shoulders. **Fort Hemenway Manor** and the **Pines Motel** offer a **courtesy shuttle** back to Heyburn for guests. Since these are courtesy shuttles, they are more or less at the owner's convenience. There are also **paid shuttle** options. See *Service Providers* on page 110. Arrangements for all shuttles need to be made in advance. This guide will describe what to expect if you are cycling to Heyburn, but first, let's take a tour of St. Maries.

Point of Interest: An entry in the Federal Writers' Project of 1950 describes St. Maries as "sprawled on hills and almost lost to itself." The remote quality noted by the writer persists. It makes the visitor to St. Maries feel as though they have stepped back a few decades in time. The city has no big box stores and there isn't even a stoplight. The people here are friendly and they love their family-centered rural lifestyle.

For **Harvest Foods** grocery store and **Riverbend Laundry**, turn left onto State Route 3 (SR-3) from Milwaukee Rd. The owner of Harvest Foods, Chester, says it's okay for cycle travelers to come in and use the **restroom**, which is right inside the main entrance. He also lets people **park their RVs** in the lot when they are riding the trails, but they need to contact him to make arrangements in advance by calling 208.245. 6555. Harvest Foods is a full-service **grocery store** with a section of handy cycle-sized **camping items** on a display near the deli. They carry things like mosquito sticks, tent pole repair kits, and fire starter—items you

St. Maries, Idaho

may have needed when camping up The Joe. Check out the historic photos on the walls. The "River through the Lakes" mural on the side of the building is one of seventeen around town that depict scenes from St. Maries' past. The Riverbend **Laundry** on the other end of the Harvest Foods parking lot is open 24 hours.

Casa de Oro Restaurant, St. Maries Golf Course

There is a **Casa de Oro** Mexican Restaurant tucked against a hillside on the southern edge of town. Dine inside or on the deck overlooking the St. Maries Golf Course and a **scenic** back-drop of beautiful mountains. Take SR-3 south .4 mile and turn left up Golf Course Rd. It's uphill for about a mile to the nicest restaurant in town, and worth the effort.

Owner, Marco, says the *Arroz con Pollo, Pollo con Crema*, and *Carne Asada*, are among the most popular dishes. They are traditional family recipes brought from Jalisco, Mexico. The menu includes hamburgers for those desiring American fare. There is a full-service lounge here. Summer hours are 11 a.m. to 10 p.m, with a daily lunch special for $5.95 year-round. Call 208.245.3200.

There is **year-round mountain biking** at Christmas Hills Recreation Area, a multi-use trail system in the hills west of the Golf Course. Tom Miller, from The Bike Shop at Hughes Ace Hardware, grooms some of the trails for winter fat biking. There is an annual fat bike group ride at Christmas Hills on Groundhog Day, or the nearest Sunday. Tom says it has what may very well be the longest name in cycling: the *Murmeltiertagfettfahrradsfest*, German for *Groundhog Day Fat Bicycle Fest*. If you have questions about how to go join the ride, call Tom at 208.245.6544.

To reach downtown St. Maries, ride west on the bridge over the St. Maries River toward **Archie's IGA**, which has a **Subway** inside. You will also see **Zips** here. That is the extent of fast food in St. Maries. Apparently there is an ordinance against it and these two are exceptions. The street becomes College Ave. Turn right onto First for the **River Front Suites** on the St. Joe River.

Each of the fully furnished and non-smoking suites can accommodate four to six people. They are spacious and cozy with **rustic log furni-**

St. Maries, Idaho

ture, futons, 32" flat screen TVs with DirectTV and DVD Player, free Wifi, complete **kitchens**, and beautiful **river views** with public docks on the St. Joe River right outside the door. If you are traveling with a dog, let them know when reserving, so they can put you in the doggie room.

There is a pleasant 15-mile out and back ride along the St. Maries River, heading south on First. The pavement ends two miles out. It is mostly flat with a few short hills the last three miles. At 7.7 miles, go left at the fork to enjoy beautiful spots along the river.

Point of Interest: St. Maries was occupied by federal troops when martial law was declared to quell union protests over harsh conditions in the lumber camps. You can read about it on the interpretive sign at the corner of College and First.

Bud's Burgers, a half block west, is a favorite among the locals for breakfast, plus, you can still get a burger there for $5. They also offer homemade pies and serve a bean veggie burger made from scratch. The **Junction Drive-In**, one block east, has burgers, sandwiches, Mexican-style food, and ice cream treats. Check out the vintage "Order-

Stay in St. Maries **Outdoor Recreation Headquarters**

Photo Courtesy of Gazzette-Record

Race the Joe 2015
Memorial Day Weekend

A visit to friendly St. Maries (pronounced "Mary's") is like stepping back in time. This historic logging town is unpretentious and down to earth, and you won't find any big box stores, or even a stoplight, here. You can consider this the gateway to recreation in the

Paul Bunyan Days
Labor Day Weekend

St. Joe National Forest, where miles of scenic backcountry beckon with outdoor activities such as: camping, floating, hiking, hunting, fishing, berry picking, mountain biking, snowriding, gem hunting, and whitewater rafting. So join the fun!

Visitors come to St. Maries to **dig star garnets** at Emerald Creek Garnet Area, 30 miles south on Hwy 3, near Clarkia. It's one of only two places on earth where these rare gems have been discovered. Unearth **Fossils** also, two miles south of Clarkia at the Fossil Bowl.

The city's logging roots run deep here. They are commemorated at the Logger Memorial on the east end of Main St. and Mullan Park on the west entrance of town. Play a round of golf at St. Maries' scenic 9-hole course, swim in the river at Aqua Park, and take the self-guided walking tour of 17 historic murals around town.

Race the Joe! Jet Boat Races ~ Motorcycle Races
Rattitude Rod Rumble ~ Paul Bunyan Days

Check the Web site for updates on these events & more throughout the year!

St. Maries Chamber of Commerce

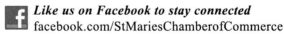

Like us on Facebook to stay connected
facebook.com/StMariesChamberofCommerce

208-245-3563 stmarieschamber.org

PO Box 162, St. Maries, Idaho 83861
manager@stmarieschamber.org

St. Maries, Idaho

Matic." If you turn right over the bridge at the Junction Drive-In, then take the first left, you will see a sign for **swimming** and **picnicing**. The left turn to the riverside **Aqua Park** is just past the sign.

To stay at **Fort Hemenway Manor**, continue west on College. You will come upon Benewah County Courthouse on the right, a building on the National Register of Historic Places, with the Ten Commandments still on the lawn. There are **pubic restrooms** downstairs. The auto licensing office in the right corner of the lobby has St. Maries' best display of **historical photos** from the steamboat and logging days. The friendly clerks don't mind when visitors stop in just to view the pictures. The **post office** is one block south of the courthouse on Seventh St. For the **St. Maries Library** with free **Wifi,** continue west on College another block. To reach the manor, turn left on Ninth St., ride south one block to Jefferson, then turn right one block to Tenth St.

Fort Hemenway Manor commands a stately presence on the corner of Tenth and Jefferson. The home was completed in 1913 for lumber baron Fred Hemenway and features beveled glass windows, custom English chandeliers, oak floors with intricate walnut inlay, beamed ceilings, a fireplace trimmed with Italian tile, and antique furnishings throughout.

A tasteful blend of present and past, you may enjoy a movie in the entertainment room, or gather in the formal living room where a guest might perform an impromptu number on the upright grand piano. Rest in one of four beautifully appointed rooms, where bed sheets are pressed in an antique mangle. Absorb tranquil views of the surrounding Bitterroot Mountains from any of the bedrooms or from a shady spot on the porch.

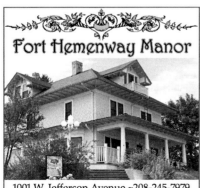

1001 W. Jefferson Avenue ~208-245-7979
forthemenwaymanor.com

In the morning your hostess, Gigi, will prepare a full-course gourmet **breakfast** with selections such as: huckleberry scones, fire roasted veggie frittata, tabouli scrambled eggs, or apple stuffed French toast. There is **free Internet** in the manor, and **secure bicycle storage** is inside on the lower level. There is also a furnished studio option downstairs for short or long-term stays. If a

St. Maries, Idaho

courtesy shuttle between the Trail of the Coeur d'Alenes and St. Maries is desired, please inquire when making reservations.

Look down the hill on Tenth to see the main entrance to **Aqua Park** in the distance. You can **swim** there in the St. Joe River and have lunch at a **picnic** table. The **restroom** at the gate is open seasonally.

Point of Interest: If you take Tenth St. to Aqua Park, you will pass the **historic railroad depot**, built in 1908. The main line of the Chicago, Milwaukee, and Puget Sound Railroad came through until 1980. The **interpretive sign** notes the townfolk's

The gate in the dike at St. Maries Aqua Park can be closed in the event of flooding

displeasure with the modest design of the building.

St. Maries once had a bustling business district along the waterfront. Steamboats pulled in three times a day, dropping off and picking up people and freight. The local Indians sometimes boarded with their horses. The Joe was a popular destination for well-dressed travelers from Spokane, who went by train to Coeur d'Alene, then took the steamers for relaxing daytrips up the St. Joe River. The excursions often included dancing by moonlight on the return trip.

You can also go down Tenth to find St. Maries' full service bicycle repair and rental shop. Turn right one block north of Main Ave, on Center, and look for Ace Hardware between Ninth and Tenth. **The Bike Shop at Hughes Ace** is on the lower level of the hardware store

St. Maries, Idaho

and there is a door in the back alley where you can wheel right in. Bikes can be dropped off and picked up anytime Ace is open, even if the bike shop is closed. Call 208.245.6544 for details and shop hours.

The Bike Shop is an authorized *Specialized* and *Redline* dealer that offers a full range of **cycles and accessories**. Tom Miller has more than 25 years professional bike repair experience, and he is trained for **custom fitting** whatever bike you ride. He is also an avid cyclist who is happy to share tips about good local rides. He is the one to talk to about biking at Christmas Hills. The Bike Shop also sponsors the **White Pine Pedal Mettle Citizens' Ride** south of St. Maries on the White Pine Scenic Byway (SR-3). Various options range from 15 to 111 miles. Get details at pedalmettle.com or call Tom at the shop.

Start early if you want to browse the stores on Main Ave., because most close shortly after 5 p.m. so the proprietors can spend time with their families. Likewise, most places are closed Sundays.

Back on Main and Tenth, **E**spresso and **wines** are available at **The Brickwall Spa**, an eclectic beauty salon with a twist. They sell espresso and wine, and sometimes host live music events. The **Handy Corner** restaurant across the street opens daily at 5 a.m. for early birds, and a large variety of breakfasts are served all day. They also offer a whopping variety of 51 burgers, from their *All American Cheese Burger*, to a *YUK Burger* with peanut butter and bacon. The YUK was purportedly one of Elvis Presley's favorites. (This area was once home to a popular Elvis impersonator, who also delivered mail around town). **The Paperhouse,** across the street and a half block east, carries a good selection of books on **local history**. Stop in there also to see the **Gallery on Main**, which features a small display of works by area jewelers, scultptors, and painters.

Main Street Bistro & Espresso two doors east, is a blend of two St. Maries businesses now combined at this location: Hill's Cabin City Pizza and Main Street Antiques & Espresso. They still offer the full selection of **espresso** flavors, **homemade fudge**, **Dreyers ice cream** and the free **Wifi**. Now there is also a menu of **pizzas** (from personal to supreme) with vegetarian, **gluten free**, and thin crust options; and pasta boats with choices of seafood and chicken alfredo, chicken pesto, sausage pepper bake, lasagna, and crab ravioli. There are five varieties of wraps, five kinds of salad, soup, bread sticks, a small selection of sandwiches, and **beer and wine** offerings. This downtown business is open daily year round from 7 a.m. to at least 8 p.m., maybe longer.

St. Maries, Idaho

Cycle down the hill on Main to the **Hughes House Museum** to see the 1902 log cabin that served as a men's club, then as the home and office of Doc. Thompson. Check out the one-of-a-kind organ built during a span of six years by Ingvald Brown with whatever materials he had on hand, including old sewing machine parts, a baby buggy, cans, wood scraps, and rubber bands. An Idaho Ponderosa Pine tree in the yard was grown from a seed that took a trip to outer space. The museum opens in summer Wed. through Sun., 12 to 4 p.m., "if the volunteers can make it," as the brochure says. Local gardeners sell their wares at a small **farmer's market** next to the museum on Friday afternoons.

MAIN STREET Bistro & Espresso

Gifts • Cards

Pizzas
Wraps
Pasta Boats
Sandwiches
Salads
Soups

Beer & Wine
Ice Cream
Espresso
Fudge

OPEN
DAILY
7 am-8 pm

806 Main Ave, St. Maries, ID
208-245-5539

Point of Interest: The Milwaukee, St. Paul, Puget Sound railroad car at the Hughes House commemorates the line that came through between 1909 and 1980. It is a reminder of St. Maries' heyday, when thousands of rugged lumberjacks rode trains bound for the woods to work in what has been called "the most dangerous occupation in America." On a typical day you would have seen a hundred such men on the streets of St. Maries, uniformly dressed in woolen shirts and hats, mackinaws, and wool pants "sawed off" at the tops of caulked boots.

The **Logger Memorial**, a block east of the museum on Main Ave., honors those who lost their lives in the most dangerous profession. Lumber built St. Maries and it is still a major force of the economy here. The city is fiercely proud of its heritage, evident by the logging themed roadside attractions and historical photos displayed around town, in stores, at the courthouse, pictured on some of the 17 murals, and commemorated during the annual Paul

St. Maries, Idaho

Bunyan days celebration on Labor Day weekend. More of the lumbering history is enshrined at **Mullan Trail Park,** which you will encounter by going west on Main Ave., past the Paul Bunyan statue that has towered over the grade school and neighborhood since 1967.

The Pines Motel is on Main and Twelfth St. right across from the **city park** and **pool**. St. Maries' only motel has clean, quiet, air conditioned rooms, each with a mini-fridge, microwave, flat screen cable TV, phone, free Wifi, and firm beds. **Free coffee** and hot chocolate are available any time. The entire motel is **smoke-free**. Ask about a **courtesy shuttle** to the Trail of the Coeur d'Alenes in Heyburn State Park when making reservations.

The statue of John Mullan is one of six in Idaho that commemorate the building of the Mullan Military Road

To continue your trek on the Bitterroot Loop, go west on Main, past Paul Bunyan, and ride uphill for several blocks to Mullan Trail Park. The "steam donkey" here is an example of a sort of generator fueled with wood or oil that was hauled into the woods to run a cable used to skid logs. This steam donkey once operated in the Hobo Creek area, up Marble Creek. There is also a large kiosk in a gazebo with an **interpretive display** about timber stands in the St. Joe Valley and early years of logging. The **restroom** is open seasonally. Water spigots in the park are locked up, so better stock up on snacks and water *before* heading up the hill. There is no word as of this writing if the restaurant and c-store will reopen at Cabin City.

St. Joe Riverfront B&B

Continue west on SR-5 and if lodging at **St. Joe Riverfront Bed and Breakfast**, turn right on Shepherd Rd. 2.8 miles past the Steam Donkey. Ride over Cherry Creek and proceed for .5 mile. The main attraction of this spacious and comfortable B&B is the river—for a dip, or just to enjoy the scenery through the floor to ceiling windows. Pamper yourself after a long ride on the trail with king and queen beds, **balconies**, cable TV, air conditioning, and free wireless Internet. You'll get a **really good breakfast** here. Start your morning with huckleberry-strawberry stuffed French toast or veggie frittatas. The fruits and vegetables come from the garden, and the huckleberries are picked fresh in the surrounding mountains. There is room for ten guests at this inn, which make it a great choice for a group. 208.245.8687, stjoeriverbb.com.

Back on SR-5, there is a turn-off 8.1 miles out of St. Maries to one of three campgrounds in Heyburn State Park. This campground on the lake has tent and **RV camping** on a first come first served basis. Turn right onto Benewah Creek Rd. and go a little more than a mile from the highway. Call 208.686.1308. Cell service is spotty along this part of the route, so make calls at the turnout a mile back before coming down the hill.

A tenth of a mile past Benewah Creek Rd. is **Alvin's RV Park** on the left, where you can park an RV, reserve the **camping cabin**, or pitch a tent. The cabin has a table and chairs, and bunkbeds. You will need to provide your own bedding. Guests can **shower** free, do **laundry**, and use the free **wifi**. Bring food because there are no services nearby.

Point of Interest: As you ride toward Rocky Point, note the grass growing in the lake with watery paths cut through it. The grass is wild rice, which is not native to the area, but was planted several decades ago by waterfowl hunters to improve habitat. St. Maries Wild Rice Co. (now based in Oregon) harvests the certified organic rice in September and sells it online and through various distributors.

A plant that *is* native to the lake area is the water potato, which Coeur d'Alene tribal families traditionally harvest in October.

As the road hugs the lakeshore, Chatcolet Bridge will soon come into view. 2.3 miles after Benewah Campground you will come to a sign that explains how the St. Joe River flows between two lakes, and that it's the highest navigable river in the world. The elevation here is 2,307 ft. After an-

other 1.8 miles, look for the **Rocky Point** day use area on the lake. It's part of Heyburn State Park and a nice place to take a break.

Trail Miles: 177.7 Rocky Point Day Use Area
ELEVATION: 2,128 FT.

DRIVING DIRECTIONS: From I-90 take HWY 95 south 32 miles to SR-5. Head east seven miles to the park entrance. You may want to turn left on Chatcolet Rd. at six miles to get a parking permit.

AMENITIES: Restroom/Accessible, Water, Picnic Area, Interpretive Signs, Parking/ADA/RV, Swimming, Rentals, Seasonal C-Store. **Next Stop: 1 mile**

Ride a mile past Rocky Point, and turn right to Chatcolet Rd. for Heyburn State Park Headquarters. It's another 1.2 miles to complete the loop at Indian Cliffs. If you came down from Plummer you've got a 6-mile uphill ride still ahead. A big congratulations to those who rode the 300k Bitterroot Loop! Come back soon with your friends and family!

THE BITTERROOT LOOP
Service Providers

Information About Area Cycle Trails

Trail of the Coeur d'Alenes/The Coeur d'Alenes Old Mission State Park, Kathleen Durfee, Manager–208.682.3814. OLD@idpr.idaho.gov parksandrecreation.idaho.gov
Trail of the Coeur d'Alenes/Coeur d'Alene Tribe, Jason Brown, Manager–208.686.1118
Trail of the Coeur d'Alenes/Heyburn State Park, Ron Hise, Ranger–208.686.1308
South Lake Promotions, Inc.; southlakecda.com/trail.htm
Friends of the Coeur d'Alene Trails; friendsofcoeurdalenetrails.org
Spokane Centennial Trail–509.624.7188; spokanecentennialtrail.org
North Idaho Centennial Trail–208.292.1634; www.northidahocentennialtrail.org
Route of the Hiawatha–208.744.1301; www.skilookout.com

Get to the Trails Without Driving

LOCAL TRAIL TOURING SERVICE

ROW Adventures–866.836.9340; rowadventurecenter.com. Guided tours on the Trail of the Coeur d'Alenes with knowledgeable, certified interpretive guides, June 1 to Aug. 30. Learn about the Coeur d'Alene Indians, Jesuit missionaries, fur trappers, mining history, early pioneers, and more on this (approximate) 20-mile ride. Transport to/from Coeur d'Alene is included. Or select the Route of the Hiawatha full day guided tour. Alternately, ROWs 5-day Bitterroot Bonanza starts in Spokane and combines bike touring on three dedicated cycling trails, rafting on the Clark Fork River, and kayaking on Lake Coeur d'Alene. Also offered is support for your own self-guided vacation, including full logistical support with luggage transfers, lodging, and shuttles when needed. ROW is based in Coeur d'Alene, ID, and Spokane, WA. Spokane office hours are seasonal. The Coeur d'Alene center at 202 E. Sherman Ave. in Coeur d'Alene is open Mon. to Fri., 9 a.m. to 5 p.m. *National Geographic Adventure Magazine* voted ROW Adventures one of the "Best Adventure Travel Companies on Earth."

TAXIS AND SHUTTLES

Captain Lou's Bicycle Shuttle Services–208.818.2254 (Based in Harrison, ID).
Payless Airport–208.762.7433 (Can accommodate up to 7 with cycles. Call to clarify rules about how to transport bikes & make pre-arrangements).
Spokane Airport Express.–509.413.7986. They provide transports all around the region, so don't let the name fool you. They are willing to explore all cyclist transport needs. Prefer you call two days in advance, but will do shorter time if logistics allow.

BOAT TRANSPORT

Captain Lou's Bicycle Shuttle Services–208 818 2254 (Based in Harrison).
HI Water Adventures–208.245.4517 (Boat shuttle on Lake CdA for people & bikes).

PUBLIC BUSES

Spokane Area Transit–509.328.RIDE (7433) www.spokanetransit.com.
CityLink–1.877.941.RIDE (7433) www.idahocitylink.com.
Greyhound–www.greyhound.com.

NOTE: *Services providers listed in* **Bold** *support this guide and/or related Web sites. Please consider them for your cycle vacation needs.*

THE BITTERROOT LOOP
Service Providers

Cycle Equipment Rental

Excelsior Cycle, Kellogg–208.786.3751
Pedal Pushers Bike Rental and Repair, Harrison–208.689.3436
Silver Mountain Sports Shop, Kellogg–208.783.1517
Terra Sports, Coeur d'Alene–208.765.5446
The Bike Shop at Hughes Ace Hardware, St. Maries–208.245.6544
Lookout Pass–208.744.1301

Watercraft Rental

Harrison Pontoons and Rentals, Harrison–208.696.1770
HI Water Adventures, Harrison–208.245.4517

(Check with your lodgings provider to inquire about rental package deals).

Lodging and Camping–Trail of the Coeur d'Alenes

ACCOMMODATIONS WITHIN ONE MILE OF THE TRAIL

PLUMMER TRAILHEAD
Hiway Motel & Sport Shop–208.686.1205
INDIAN CLIFFS & CHATCOLET TRAILHEAD
Heyburn State Park–(Camping, Cabins & Cottages. RVs, Tents)–888.922.6743, 208.686.1308
LACON
Crow's Nest Cottage–(Vacation Home, 2 day min.)–208.696.1770
HARRISON TRAILHEAD
Cabin, The–(Vacation Home, 3 day min.)–208.661.8929
City of Harrison Campground–208.689.3393 (Seasonal Host)–208.689.3212
Corskie House B&B–208.689.9265
Harrison House–(Vacation Home, 2 day min.)–208.696.1770
Lakeview Lodge–(Motel)–208.689.9789
Osprey Inn–(B&B)–208.689.9502
CATALDO TRAILHEAD
Kahnderosa RV/Campgrounds–(RVs and Tents)–208.682.4613
The Mission Inn–(Primitive tenting)–208.682.4435
ENAVILLE TRAILHEAD
Albert's Landing–(RVs and Tents)–208.682.4179
PINE CREEK TRAILHEAD
By the Way Campground–(Camping Cabin, RVs, and Tents)–208.682.3311
KELLOGG TRAILHEAD
Guest House Inn & Suites–(Motel)–208.783.1234
Kellogg Vacation Homes–800.435.2588
Morning Star Lodge–(Silver Mt. Resort, rooms and suites)–866.344.2675
Silverhorn Motor Inn–800.437.6437
The Ridge–(Vacation Condos)–800.435.2588
Trail Motel–208.784.1161
ELIZABETH PARK TRAILHEAD
Crystal Gold Mine–(RV)–208.783.4653

Lodging and Camping–Trail of the Coeur d'Alenes

OSBURN TRAILHEAD
Blue Anchor RV Park–(RVs and Tents)–208.752.3443
WALLACE TRAILHEAD
Brooks Hotel–208.556.1571
Hercules Inn–(Vacation Rental Suites)–208.556.0575
Stardust Motel–208.752.1213
The Banker–(Vacation Home)800.435.2588
The Lux Rooms–(Boutique Hotel)–208.753.6001
The Ryan Hotel–(Boutique Hotel)–208.753.6001
The Wallace Inn–(Motel, Courtesy Shuttle)–800.643.2386
Wallace RV Park–(Camping Cabins, RVs, and Tents)–208.753.7121
MULLAN TRAILHEAD
Lookout Motel–208.744.1601
Mullan House B&B–208.755.8547
Mullan Trail–(Cabins, RVs)–208.744.1444

Lodging and Camping–Northern Pacific (NorPac)

LOOKOUT PASS
Lookout Pass Ski & Recreation Area–(Self Contained RV)–208.744.1301

Lodging and Camping–Old Milwaukee Road

NORTH FORK ST JOE (Between Pearson Trailhead and Avery, Idaho)
Telichpah Forest Service Campground–208.245.4517
AVERY, IDAHO
Avery Gift Shop–(Vacation Suite)–208.245.1308, or 208.245.2055
Cabins by the Joe–Cabins, RV Camping–425.773.3725
Scheffy's Hotel–208.245.4410
MARBLE CREEK TRAILHEAD–(Between Avery and Calder)
St. Joe Lodge–(Rooms)–208.245-2284
CALDER, IDAHO
Calder Store–(RVs, Primitive Tenting)–208.245-2284

Lodging and Camping–State Route Five

ST. MARIES, IDAHO
Birch Tree B&B–208.245.2198 or 208.691.3696
Fort Hemenway Manor–(B&B, Courtesy Shuttle)–208.245.7979
River Front Suites–208.582.1724
St. Joe Riverfront Bed & Breakfast–208.245.8687
The Guest House–208.245.5755
The Pines Motel–(Courtesy Shuttle) 208.245.2545

BETWEEN ST MARIES AND PLUMMER
Alvin's Campground–(RVs, Tents, Camping Cabin)–208.245.5879
Heyburn State Park, Benewah–(RVs, Tents)–208.686.1308
Heyburn State Park, Hawley's–(Cottages, Cabins, RVs, Tents)–208.686.1308

THE BITTERROOT LOOP
Service Providers

Lodging and Camping-Bitterroot Loop

OTHER ACCOMMODATIONS–MORE THAN A MILE OFF THE TRAILS

HARRISON MARINA TRAILHEAD
    Grandma's Cabin–(Vacation Home on Trail). Mostly flat 5-mile ride on rural highway and lakeside road.–208.696.1770.

BULL RUN TRAILHEAD
    Watson's Rose Lake Resort–(Vacation Apartment, Rustic Cabins, RV, Tenting). Mostly flat 2-mile ride on rural highway.–208.682.3604.

EAST PORTAL, ROUTE OF THE HIAWATHA
    Mangold's General Store and Motel, Saltese, MT. Flat ride of 4.2 miles on multi-use trail.–406.678.4328

BETWEEN AVERY AND CALDER
    Spring Creek Cabins–(Camping cabins). 2-mile flat ride on hwy.–208.245.5268

Connecting Trips: Trail of the Coeur d'Alenes

Connecting Trips present additional options for food, lodging, and/or recreation. These destinations are selected for their unique features or services, even though they are more than a mile from the Bitterroot Loop trails. All but one have lodgings on site or close by. To qualify as a Connecting Trip they must be:
    1) Fun or intereseting.
    2) Be accessiblesible by an easy, primarily flat ride from a trailhead, or, offer a courtesy shuttle or other transport option.
These Connecting Trips are listed by trailhead from west to east, (clockwise) on the Bitterroot Loop.

CHATCOLET TRAILHEAD
    H2H Bison Ranch & RV Camp–(Dry Cabins, RV, Tenting, Food Option, Courtesy Shuttle)–208.686.0108, h2hbisonranch.com
    Sun Meadow Family Nudist Resort–(Motel Rooms, Cabin, RV, Tenting, Food, Courtesy Shuttle)–208.686.8686, sunmeadow.org

CATALDO TRAILHEAD
    Coeur d'Alenes Old Mission State Park–(Historical Attraction)–208.682.3814 parksandrecreation.idaho.gov/parks/coeur-d-alenes-old-mission

ENAVILLE TRAILHEAD
    Country Lane B&B Resort on the North Fork–(B&B, Cabin, RV, Tenting, Food, Courtesy Shuttle)–1.877.670.5927, countrylaneresort.com

SILVER MOUNTAIN TRAILHEAD
    Silver Mt. Resort–(Gondola Ride, Mountain Activities, Food)–877.230.2193, silvermt.com

Government Offices

Coeur d'Alene Tribe–208.686.1800; Tribal Police–208.686.2050
Benewah County–208.245.3212; Sheriff, non-emergency–208.245.2555
Kootenai County–208.446.1000; Sheriff, non-emergency–208.446.1300
Shoshone County–208.752.1264; Sheriff, non-emergency–208.556.1114
Idaho Panhandle National Forests Headquarters–208.765-7233

EMERGENCY: DIAL 9-1-1

THE BITTERROOT LOOP
Roadside Attractions

- ☐ The Veterans' Memorial, Plummer Trailhead
- ☐ *Smoke Signals* Movie Location, Bobbi's Bar, Plummer
- ☐ Historic Mullan Military Rd., Heyburn State Park, Plummer
- ☐ Chatcolet Bridge, Heyburn State Park
- ☐ Longest Electrical Cable, Over South Lake Coeur d'Alene
- ☐ Old Harrison Jail, Crane Museum, Harrison
- ☐ Historic Building Walking Tour, Harrison
- ☐ Idaho's Oldest Building, Coeur d'Alenes Old Mission, Cataldo
- ☐ *Dante's Peak* Movie Location, Albert's Landing, Enaville
- ☐ Building Wearing a Miner's Hat, Kellogg
- ☐ North America's Longest Gondola, Silver Mountain, Kellogg
- ☐ Scrap Metal Sculptures, Kellogg
- ☐ WPA Historic Post Office Mural, Kellogg
- ☐ 1882 Underground Gold Mine, Crystal Gold Mine, Kellogg
- ☐ Sunshine Mine Disaster Memorial, Big Creek
- ☐ Captain John Mullan Statue, Wallace
- ☐ Center of the Universe, Historic Downtown Wallace
- ☐ *Dante's Peak* Movie Location, Historic Downtown Wallace
- ☐ *Heaven't Gate* Movie Location, Historic Downtown Wallace
- ☐ Historic Trolley Rides and Mine Tour, Wallace
- ☐ Last Stop Light in a Coffin, Wallace Mining Museum, Wallace
- ☐ Mining Display, Wallace Visitor Center, Wallace
- ☐ Pulaski Monument, Wallace
- ☐ Elmer's Fountain, along I-90 Near Mullan
- ☐ Captain John Mullan Statue, Mullan
- ☐ Avery Jail, Downtown Avery
- ☐ Milwaukee Dining Car, Downtown Avery
- ☐ Trout Pond, Downtown Avery
- ☐ Historic Logging Display, Marble Creek on the St. Joe River
- ☐ Captain John Mullan Statue, St. Maries
- ☐ Historic Murals, Downtown St. Maries
- ☐ Logger Memorial, Downtown St. Maries
- ☐ Paul Bunyan Statue, Downtown St. Maries
- ☐ Steam Donkey, Mullan Park, St. Maries
- ☐ Outer Space Tree, Hughes House, Downtown St. Maries
- ☐ World's Highest Navigable River, State Route 5
- ☐ Civilian Conservation Corps Projects, Heyburn State Park